Female of the Species

Wensley Clarkson

BLAKE'S
TRUE
CRIME
LIBRARY

Published by Blake Publishing Ltd,
3 Bramber Court, 2 Bramber Road,
London W14 9PB, England

364·152

First published in 2000

ISBN 1 85782 348 6

British Library Cataloguing-in-Publication Data:
A catalogue record for this book is available
from the British Library.

Typeset by t2

Printed in Finland by
WSOY

1 3 5 7 9 10 8 6 4 2

Contents

Dear Reader

In his first volume for Blake's True Crime Library, *Deadlier than the Male*, Wensley Clarkson took us straight into the heart of the most horrific crimes and into the minds of the most notorious criminals. In this second volume, he delves even further into the female criminal psyche...

Take the ex-nun turned stripper, who ended up on a deadly murder charge; or the Nazi victim who would stop at nothing to reclaim what was rightfully hers; or even the ex-policewoman who, consumed with jealousy, took a walk on the other side of the law when she wreaked terrible vengeance upon her rival in love.

Seldom has there been such a compellingly eerie collection of tales. They would not be out of place in a book of the most sinister fiction — and yet every word you will read in this book is true.

Adam Parfitt
Editor
Blake's True Crime Library

Deadly Threesome

The throbbing sound of a heavy bass guitar thudded through the club and a cloud of blue smoke hung over the stage. Then she appeared, wearing a full nun's habit and balancing precariously near the edge of the raised surface, her face soft, round, yet stern, dark brown eyes staring out into the blackness in front of her. Gradually, she built up speed. Faster, faster she danced, then gave a glance across to the other corner of the dimly-lit club.

She looked at her watch for a split second and then began her routine as though demons were lurking somewhere within her, her dark, swept-back hair hidden by the nun's head-dress.

Then she caught sight of him, sneering in the far corner by the bar, a beer in one hand and a cigarette in the other. He was staring right at her and she knew precisely what was going through his mind.

As she lifted the nun's habit to reveal her long, stocking-clad legs to a murmur from the audience, she saw her best friend Bonnie sliding alongside that man by the bar. It enraged her. Sickened her. Incensed her. She ripped open the front of her outfit with fury, although to the audience of men it looked like a well-choreographed move.

Aud Hegesanti was outraged that he was there watching her. She was even more infuriated that Bonnie had gone up to him. It made her sick to the stomach. 'Come on. Show us more!' shouted a voice in the crowd.

That snapped her out of her bitter and twisted mood. She unhooked her bra and peeled the stockings off her legs before running them back and forth between her teeth, much to the delight of the audience.

Aud had become something of a major attraction in Oslo, Norway, not a place normally associated with strip clubs and sleazy clip joints. The reason was that her nun routine was only one step away from the truth for the buxom brunette. Only a few months previously, the twenty-one-year-old stripper had caused a hell of a stir by joining the club after seeing off her life as a real nun in Rome.

Her story of sexual abuse at the hands of the evil elderly sisters at the nunnery made front-page news across Norway, a conservative country where such salacious goings-on rarely occur. The media were particularly fascinated by her strip routine in which she used the same habit she had worn only a few months previously to pray in. She even claimed that the way she danced for those men was similar to the type of things those awful nuns made her do as an abused teenager in Rome. It was a strip club manager's dream come true. Some nights even perfectly ordinary and respectable members of Oslo's middle class lined up at the various clubs in the hope of seeing Aud's famous routine.

However, what the papers did not mention was that Aud's vows of celibacy were soon forgotten once she joined the strip-club circuit in Norway. It transpired that the sexual depravity she suffered at the hands of those old nuns in Rome had aroused sexual preferences the young woman did not know she possessed. She rapidly became more interested in her shapely fellow dancers than in the men who filled the clubs across Oslo to see her remove her nun's habit.

The first object of Aud's genuine affection was

Bonnie — a beautiful blonde dancer whose body was the envy of virtually all the other strippers she worked alongside. At first, Bonnie had been reluctant to take up Aud's offer of friendship because she had a longtime boyfriend called Klaus. However, Aud was very persistent and charming and she seemed genuinely to care about Bonnie.

Unfortunately, Bonnie feared that Klaus — who made a habit of turning up unexpectedly at the clubs where Bonnie appeared — would get very angry and beat her if she showed an interest in any other man, let alone a shapely former nun. For months she rejected Aud's continual attempts at seduction, convinced that bisexuality just wasn't her scene. But all the time she continued to feel sorry for Aud and she also knew that certain passions were being stirred every time she talked to the ex-nun.

Then one day Klaus came into a club where Bonnie was appearing and caught Aud stroking her friend's arm as the two women sat giggling at the bar between acts. He immediately realised what was happening but, instead of getting angry, he became very intrigued.

Bonnie was embarrassed and tried to explain to Klaus that Aud had never got any further than touching her arm. Klaus was disappointed and told his lover, 'I don't mind. Why don't you bring her home tonight?'

Bonnie was appalled at her boyfriend's attitude and angrily walked away from him. Later, after they were reconciled and were on their way back to Klaus's flat, he turned on Bonnie.

'What the hell is the matter with you. If she wants to make love to you that's fine by me. Just make sure I'm included.'

'You're sick,' replied a very disillusioned Bonnie.

That night Klaus would not stop going on about his wish to see his girlfriend make love with another woman. Bonnie was getting increasingly angry.

'If you don't stop it, I am going to leave. I've had enough,' she told him.

Klaus exploded. He launched into a vicious tirade about how Bonnie wouldn't even have a roof over her head if it had not been for him. And in any case what was the harm in a little innocent fun?

Bonnie shouted back at him yet again and this time Klaus smashed her in the face very hard. She fled to the spare room and refused to come out for the rest of the evening.

Next day, Bonnie was still feeling extremely bitter about the way Klaus had treated her. She hid the bruise on her face with make-up but could not hide the hurt she felt inside. She just did not like the way he wanted her to make love to Aud while he watched. It did not seem right.

At the club that evening she met Aud and told her

all about Klaus's behaviour. Aud was a sympathetic listener. She told Bonnie that she respected her opinions on her own sexuality, but what had happened with Klaus was the precise reason why she preferred the company of women to men.

After their performances on stage that night, Aud asked Bonnie if she wanted to have a nightcap at her home, an isolated farmhouse on the outskirts of Oslo. Bonnie, desperate not to go home to face another night of violence at the hands of Klaus, accepted the offer, knowing full well what might happen.

Within a few minutes of getting to Aud's house, the two women were making warm, sensuous, caring love with each other and Bonnie admitted she did not know why she had put up with those sick and twisted men in the first place.

Aud was not a pushy, brutish 'bull-dyke' type at all. She had suffered so badly at the hands of those depraved nuns in Rome that she knew full well that gentle patience was probably the most important single ingredient when it came to enjoyable sex.

As the two women lay together in bed following hours of passion, Bonnie started to worry about Klaus. He was virtually her pimp and she feared that because she had not gone home that night he would beat her — or even worse. He had always threatened to get her if she did not do exactly as he told her. She knew that her actions would invite very big problems.

Aud was desperate to reassure the girl she had fallen deeply in love with and made a suggestion that stunned Bonnie for a few moments — until she began to consider its implications. For Aud had said that they should lay a trap for the perverted, brutal Klaus.

'Let's give him exactly what he wants and then get him out of our lives for ever. It would be justice well done. He deserves it,' explained Aud.

The next day, Klaus looked as pleased as punch when Bonnie explained to him where she had been the previous night.

'I told you that you'd enjoy it. Now I want to come and watch next time you go with her.'

'Let's do it tonight then,' said Bonnie.

Klaus kissed Bonnie full on the lips. Just the thought of his girlfriend making love to another woman in front of him was the source of great sexual excitement. He forced his tongue into her mouth. She swallowed and did not resist because she knew she would get her revenge that evening.

That night Aud, Bonnie and Klaus enjoyed a few drinks together and some playful flirtation in the corner of the bar at the club where they were stripping before heading off for Aud's remote farmhouse.

As they got out of the taxi and stumbled up the driveway, Aud whispered in Bonnie's ear, 'Don't forget we're in control.'

Within minutes of getting inside the house, Klaus

was making it perfectly clear why he had agreed to come back with the two women. He was also being particularly pushy.

'Into the bedroom now,' he grunted at them.

The two women giggled girlishly and pranced into the main bedroom. Once inside they happily performed a very private striptease for their one 'customer'.

Soon the two women were completely wrapped up in each other and virtually ignoring the panting, naked figure lying on the bed watching them.

To start with, Klaus was perfectly content enjoying his voyeuristic feast. Soon, however, he began to want more than just his own private lesbian sex show. As the two women wrapped themselves in each other, he crept quietly behind Aud and tried to have sex with her.

She immediately stopped and turned to face him.

'Get your hands off me, you woman beater.'

Klaus smiled. He did not get it. He thought she was just mocking him as part of some sick and twisted sexual game. He tried to fondle her again.

'I told you! Get away!'

With that Klaus turned to his one-time girlfriend Bonnie.

'Come on, Bonnie. I want to join in.'

Bonnie did not reply. Instead she beckoned him towards her. Both women had a glazed, deadened look in their eyes. He presumed they were inviting him to take part in an orgy. The two women played with Klaus like two kittens with a mouse. They taunted him and teased him and let him watch them only to stop their love making just before the actual moment of climax. They would not allow him to touch them. All the time the two women encouraged him to drink as many beers as he could consume. Soon he would have been incapable of sex even if they had offered it on a plate.

Eventually, Klaus's eyelids began to be more closed than open and both women knew that the time was fast approaching. When he collapsed in a drunken heap they got to work.

Klaus never even noticed Bonnie move towards him as Aud came up behind him. Bonnie sat naked in front of him just in case he awoke while Aud grasped his neck and began to squeeze. He awoke in a state of total confusion and tried to fight back, but Bonnie punched him hard in the groin and he doubled up in agony. Then she aimed a little lower. That was the place where she really wanted to inflict pain.

'We are going to teach you a lesson you'll never forget,' said Bonnie before punching him again and again.

Aud held on tight, squeezing every ounce of life out of the crumpled naked man at her feet. It was almost as if he was grovelling for his life but both women had already decided there would be only one possible outcome.

The energy was being choked out of him. The two women were breathing fast and hard now, slightly aware that a definite sense of excitement was being caused by this merciless act of violence. Neither of them felt any guilt, just quiet satisfaction that a man who expected them to perform like sex dolls at his whim was getting his just 'reward'. Moments later they extinguished the life from Klaus and toasted their everlasting love for one another in an outrageous night of love making.

Aud and Bonnie were arrested by Oslo police in November 1994, and charged with the murder of Klaus. Their trial is expected to take place in the summer of 1995.

Driven to Death

Driving instructor Ancell Marshall was renowned as a very calm character who took everything in his stride. He had a friendly demeanour but he never wavered from the job at hand. He firmly believed in gently coaxing his pupils so that they gained confidence, and then driving skills would naturally follow.

Ancell even prided himself on never having raised his voice to a pupil. Certainly there had been moments when his life seemed in peril but Ancell had always calmly taken over the controls and avoided disaster. In the words of one of his fellow teachers, he was 'a complete professional'.

So when attractive brunette Rene Sampat enrolled for a series of lessons, Ancell understandably presumed that he was about to embark on another successful mission to teach someone how to drive. When Rene got in the driver's seat to begin her first lesson, Ancell gave no thought to the friendly smile on her face or the momentary flash of thigh that she provided while adjusting her position.

Rene Sampat, who killed the wife of the man she became obsessed with.

Ancell made it a strict rule not to talk too much to pupils, fearing it might distract them from their concentration on driving. That day, however, Rene kept asking him questions and she had the unfortunate habit of turning to talk to him rather than looking ahead at the road.

'Please keep your eyes on the road,' was about the strongest remark mild-mannered Ancell ever made. Other instructors might have been a little more blunt but Ancell believed he had a duty not to be in any way offensive to his pupils.

Rene completely ignored Ancell's request and just kept on talking, but then that was typical of Rene Sampat. Every time they stopped at a junction or traffic lights, she would turn and smile in his direction. Ancell began to notice all this but did not want to acknowledge her actions because he felt it might seem rude of him.

As Rene pulled up at the end of the lesson, Ancell felt a rather strange atmosphere. He couldn't quite put his finger on it but as a man of the world he had a horrible inkling of what was about to occur.

As he turned to get out of the car, Rene engaged Ancell in yet another banal conversation. The next thing he knew her hand was on his. He couldn't quite work out if she was making a pass at him or just being over-grateful for her lesson. He pulled his hand away and ignored the entire incident.

Ancell watched Rene walk off down the street after that lesson and decided that perhaps she did seem rather forward. On the other hand, he was probably imagining it. As a lay preacher at the Seventh Day Baptist Church in Victoria Road, Tottenham, north London, he preferred to think the best of people and tucked all other thoughts away into another part of his mind. He was actually rather annoyed with himself for even suspecting Rene's motives that day.

The following week Rene turned up for another lesson and this time she looked as if she was dressed up for a evening out at a casino. Jewellery was glittering from every finger and she had such a vast pair of earrings that Ancell wondered if they would interfere with her driving capabilities.

Just as on the previous lesson, Rene made all the conversation, despite Ancell's occasional — and highly apologetic — requests for her to keep her eyes on the road. That smile seemed to be permanently painted on Rene's face whenever she looked in Ancell's direction. It was finally dawning on him that perhaps Rene did have other things on her mind besides driving.

A few minutes before the end of that lesson, Rene Sampat tried to fondle Ancell, lost control of the car momentarily and almost crashed. To this day, Ancell has been too embarrassed to say precisely what happened but he immediately told Rene that it would be better if she was taught by another instructor.

Ancell Marshall presumed that would be the end of his association with Rene. In fact, it was only just the beginning.

Ancell got quite a surprise when he was showing congregational members to their seats one Sunday and divorcee Rene — the driving-school pupil from hell — turned up, accompanied by three of her younger children.

He gulped but acted calmly and courteously. He did not know that thirty-three-year-old Rene — a mother of five — had joined the Seventh Day Baptist Church despite being a committed Muslim. Just a few months later, he began to discover why.

'You'll have to go and see her. She's asked for you by name, Ancell,' one of Ancell's fellow lay preachers at the church told him by phone one evening.

It transpired that Rene Sampat had contacted the church asking that lay preacher Ancell should visit her home to counsel her following an incident that had occurred. Ancell's colleague said it sounded pretty serious and he had a duty to investigate.

When Ancell knocked on the front door of Rene's home in Seaford Road, he was feeling very apprehensive but the trusting side of his nature told him not to make any prejudgements. This lady had said she had been attacked and she needed gentle patience, not a suspicious response from a man who feared that her intentions might not be entirely honourable.

He sat and listened to her story of having been raped by a stranger and recommended that she call in the police, but she refused. Ancell left her home that evening rather bemused by the whole story. Nothing was ever mentioned about it again.

Then, a few months later, Rene phoned Ancell at midnight when he was in bed with his wife Jannette, just about to go to sleep. This time Rene was in tears. She told him she had been raped again and gagged and tied up and could he come round and untie her.

Ancell took a deep breath and advised her to call the police, but she refused. Again, the incident was never mentioned again, although Ancell did feel a little worried about Rene's motives in calling him in the first place.

When Ancell was told by his colleagues at the church to go round to Rene's house following a third rape allegation he became extremely apprehensive about whether he should even be going there.

Within minutes of arriving at the house, Rene burst into tears and then tried to kiss Ancell. All Ancell's worst nightmares were coming to fruition. He immediately pulled back from Rene, but she then collapsed at his feet and pleaded with him to go to bed with her there and then.

Ancell was totally confused. He could not understand how a woman would make very serious claims of rape in one breath and then ask for sex with a happily married man the next moment. He kept reminding her of his married status and the position he held in the church but Rene's obsession was not that easily extinguished.

Ancell once again advised Rene to go to the police about her rape allegations. She ignored him and insisted on talking about what they could do in bed together.

Soon afterwards, Ancell left the house in a very confused stare. He knew that any involvement with Rene would be certain to lead to even greater problems but as a lay preacher he genuinely believed that he had a duty to help her. It was hardly as if he could go to the police about her. They had more important things to deal with than a lay preacher claiming that a woman was trying to seduce him!

Rightly or wrongly, Ancell decided to let sleeping dogs lie. His only concern was to get on with his life as a driving instructor, responsible husband to a quietly-spoken wife, and father to their three children.

However, Rene was still desperate to lure Ancell into her web of seduction so she took Ancell's advice and called the police to her home in nearby Stoke Newington after another alleged 'attack'. She hoped that their involvement might actually convince Ancell that she needed sympathy and understanding.

Officers who arrived at the house were bemused to find Rene still naked and tied up. She told them a man had climbed in her window and asked her 'to do all sorts of things to him' at knifepoint.

Then, after the officers had untied her, Rene ran into the kitchen of the flat and tried to stab herself after one of the detectives suggested she might be lying. Rene only calmed down after a policeman said he had powers to take away her children if she continued acting in such an erratic manner.

Some months later, Ancell got a call from his father who also attended the same church in Tottenham. He had some disturbing news: Rene Sampat had been to visit him and had pleaded with him to convince Ancell to have an affair with her.

Ancell was shocked. His father went on to explain that Rene kept going on and on about it to him. She even said she did not want to marry his son, just to 'have a relationship with him'.

Ancell was completely astounded. How could a grown woman — and mother of five children — go and see his father and talk in such an obscene manner? It all seemed unreal and for that reason Ancell decided to do nothing about it. He did not confront Rene. He did not even act any differently when he saw her in church each Sunday. He had decided that, as the Lord's servant, he had to show compassion and forgiveness towards her. That meant making an extra-special effort to be kind to Rene just to make sure she did not feel hurt. In retrospect, Ancell Marshall should have nipped the entire situation in the bud, but he did not.

By 1987, Rene had become remarkably generous towards not only Ancell, but his entire family. Ancell was convinced that all that 'confusion' earlier had been forgotten, and if anything, Rene was trying to show that she wanted to be a genuine friend. She even sent Ancell a £70 overcoat, as well as countless gifts for his family.

And Ancell — being a highly religious and forgiving man — tried to show how much he now trusted Rene by allowing her to look after his children whenever Jannette was out working. He had no idea that she was only prepared to look after the youngsters because it gave her an opportunity to ingratiate herself with the man of her dreams.

When Jannette Marshall celebrated her birthday that year, Rene even persuaded a friend of the family to lend her the key to their flat so that she could prepare a surprise meal for Jannette and decorate a room as part of the celebrations.

Ancell was delighted by this apparent about turn on the part of Rene. All the sexual innuendo and obscene suggestions from earlier days had been completely put behind them both. He even noticed that his wife was growing increasingly fond of Rene.

However, Rene's mind was still filled with wild fantasies concerning Ancell. She was perfectly happy to put on a façade in front of his wife, just so that she could be near to the man who she actually believed could give her everlasting happiness.

Sometimes she found herself admiring him secretly from head to toe at church functions. She memorised every single detail of his body and stored it in her mind so that she could visualise them in bed together whenever she wanted.

Ancell occasionally caught a lingering glance from Rene but dismissed it as simple friendship, although it definitely did bother him. One time, she brushed past him in the kitchen at their home and, for a split second, he felt her quickening breath. Then the moment passed.

By the winter of 1988, Rene's sexual fantasies about Ancell were bordering on the dangerously obsessive. She decided that if she could not have Ancell as her secret lover, she would start a campaign to have him entirely to herself.

During a holiday in Tunisia, Rene confessed to a girlfriend — who was also a close friend of the Marshalls — that she would marry Ancell if anything ever happened to his wife. The friend was shocked by Rene's open admission of lust for Ancell.

Rene knew precisely what she was doing. She wanted to make sure her thoughts were conveyed to Mrs Marshall. She then decided to stir up even more trouble by insisting to the friend she had had an affair with Ancell and become pregnant but had had an abortion.

It was all so detailed that the friend believed her. In fact, Rene had been fantasising for so long about her 'life' with Ancell that she had virtually begun to believe in her own lies, making them sound even more convincing.

Rene openly longed to have Ancell to herself She was also desperate to have a child by him as that would seal their 'love' for one another. In her imagination she had married him already. She could visualise them making love together; bringing up children; living in a wonderful house. It would all have made a perfect Mills and Boon fantasy if it had not been so tragically misguided.

Rene's sad and twisted vision of her imaginary life with Ancell came crashing down in September 1989, when Jannette Marshall became pregnant with her fourth child. The reality of what was happening suddenly dawned on Rene and she became very angry and vindictive. How could he do such a thing to her? How could he betray her by having another child by that woman?

In Rene's mind it should have been her having that baby by Ancell. She looked on Jannette's pregnancy in much the same way a wife would look upon it if her husband's mistress was having a child. Rene believed she was the wife and Jannette was the other woman. She was starting to lose touch with reality.

A stream of nasty, vindictive, threatening, poison-pen letters began arriving at Ancell Marshall's home. He suspected they were coming from Rene but could not be sure. Jannette Marshall was naturally upset and very concerned that such a vicious person should embark on a highly personal campaign against them.

What made them doubly bizarre was that some of the letters were signed by someone calling themselves 'Erek' and they suggested that the child

Jannette Marshall was carrying was a result of an affair with 'Erek'. The letter went on to insist that Jannette preferred 'Erek' to Ancell and read:

'When you touch her body she says it feels like a snake. You breath stink. You cannot kiss good.'

Another letter claimed 'Erek' had made love to Jannette in the family home and even left a condom in the toilet.

At the Seventh Day Baptist Church, Rene secretly daubed graffiti on a wall, saying that 'Erek' was the father of the couple's latest child. People were starting to talk. Was there something going on between Rene and Ancell after all? Her campaign was starting to make inroads into his otherwise happily married life.

Ancell was stunned. How could Rene Sampat go to such extremes? But then, perhaps it wasn't her after all. He was very confused by the entire situation but still Ancell refused to go to the police, preferring to hope it would all blow over.

By the time the baby was born, the Marshalls were in an understandably distressed state as the letters continued to arrive with alarming regularity. Each time they would get more obscene.

Then one letter turned up containing the ominous threat that Jannette would die on the first birthday of the child. Ancell read it and, yet again, chose to ignore it. No one knows why Ancell never actually confronted Rene about his suspicions concerning those poison-pen letters. Instead, he allowed Rene to continue to step in and out of his life. He even hired her to cook food for a takeaway restaurant he ran as a sideline to his driving school.

In the middle of April 1991, Ancell actually visited Rene's home to collect some food she had cooked for his restaurant. For Rene, having Ancell in her home was too good an opportunity to resist. Soon, she was trying to kiss and embrace him. Ancell used the tray of food he had just picked up to push her away but Rene tried to hold him and kiss him on the mouth, pushing her tongue between his lips.

'What is the matter with you?' said Ancell and pushed her away.

Rene felt humiliated by his rejection. She had actually presumed that by coming to her house he was finally going to consummate their love for one another. She had never doubted that they would end up making love that evening. She had worked it all out in her fantasies. Instead Ancell had rejected her in a cruel and callous manner.

She decided there and then that the only way to have him for herself would involve a carefully planned scheme to get rid of her rival for his love. She began to construct a story that would guarantee her revenge on her rival.

At her home in Seaford Road, Tottenham, Rene

broke down in tears one evening and poured out her problems to her sixteen-year-old son Roy. She insisted she had been raped by a man who was ordered to attack her by Jannette Marshall. She recalled vivid details of the 'attack' and of how jealous Jannette had sworn revenge on her because of her close relationship with Ancell Marshall.

'We have to pay her back for what she has done,' Rene told Roy.

Like any good son, Roy was appalled at what his mother was saying. He agreed that they had to do something to get back at Jannette Marshall for causing this horrific attack on Rene.

She kept repeating over and over again how terrible it had been to be raped and that no one should be allowed to get away with it. Rene was cleverly manipulating the situation by playing on her son's emotions. Soon he had worked himself up into a lather of hatred for Jannette Marshall and could not wait to go round to her home and see that 'justice' was done.

On 28 April 1991, a few days before the baby's first birthday, Rene called Ancell at his takeaway restaurant and pleaded with him to visit her. 'You must call round here before you go home.' Rene was most insistent. It bothered Ancell because, despite all of her bizarre behaviour over the previous six years, she had never before been so pushy about getting him to go round to her home. However, after what had happened on the previous occasion, Ancell refused and, instead, went home to his wife Jannette and their children.

The house was pitch-dark by the time Ancell arrived home. An eerie silence enveloped the hallway. He walked into the sitting room and flicked on a light switch.

Lying on the floor was the lifeless body of his wife, Jannette. She had been strangled, beaten and stabbed fifteen times. The blanket covering her was caked in blood. Ancell was horrified. He rushed to gather up the couple's children, aged ten, eight, seven and eleven months, and then went outside and called the police on his mobile phone.

At the Old Bailey, in October 1993, Rene Sampat was jailed for life for the murder of Jannette Marshall. Her sixteen-year-old son Roy Aziz had carried out the murder after she 'manipulated and inflamed' him with false claims that the dead woman had got a man to rape her. Roy had earlier been convicted and ordered to be detained in youth custody.

Their conviction brought to an end a lengthy ordeal for Ancell Marshall, who had been arrested and had stood trial for the murder of his wife at the same court in February 1992. He was released halfway through the hearing when the judge ruled that there was no case for him to answer. Tragically, he had been refused permission to attend his wife's funeral while in custody awaiting trial.

Rene had been a prosecution witness against Ancell but a fresh police investigation uncovered the depth of her obsession, together with evidence which pointed to her hand behind the murder.

Prosecuting counsel Nigel Sweeney said at the trial: 'She was the person with the motive to set it [the murder] up. She was infatuated with him and tried in various ways over a number of years to win him over, without success. She determined that Jannette Marshall should be murdered so that Ancell could be hers.'

Ancell Marshall whispered 'amen' as the jury gave their verdict. Outside the court, however, he had to be given police protection when he was bombarded with stones by a mob supporting Rene Sampat.

He said: 'I am elated and satisfied that justice has been done. It won't bring my wife back but it was necessary that those who have committed this evil act on my wife should be brought to justice.'

Deeply religious Ancell added that he felt a 'divine intervention' had been present throughout the case. 'I feel to a certain extent it was almost necessary for me to have been treated in that manner ... almost as a scapegoat ... in order that the real person or persons responsible should be brought to justice. My prayers have been answered and I knew God would vindicate me over the horrible and nasty smear that has been said about me.

Ancell claimed he had no idea that Rene was obsessed with him. 'She is demonic and evil. She is wicked. She has referred to an obsession but I can only sum it up as saying that she has been used by the Devil.'

Ancell and his daughters Charlene, now thirteen, Naomi, now eleven, Stacey, seven and three-year-old Rebecca are currently living with his mother in another part of Tottenham.

'I often wonder why our family had to suffer this. But we're in God's hands. He must have had a reason to allow it,' he added.

Detective Superintendent Gavin Robertson, who led the investigation, said: 'The sort of woman who can plan the death of a mother of four who had never done her any harm, and use her own sixteen-year-old son to do it, is beyond words.'

Rene Sampat's QC, Mr Graham Boal, told Mr Justice Richard Lowry: 'You may think it has been realistically described as a fatal attraction and you may think it can also be described as a fatal obsession.'

As Rene Sampat was led to the cells she shouted out: 'I am not guilty of murder. I am guilty of love.'

The Green-Eyed Monster

Their eyes first met across a crowded ice-skating rink. She was just fifteen, tall, shapely and very confident. He was seventeen, awkward, shy and extremely inexperienced.

Andrew Morgan watched Jacqueline gliding gracefully over the ice and told a friend she was the prettiest girl he had ever seen. As their eyes locked for a second time, she performed a twirl on the rink just for him. He looked in wonderment at her long, slender legs and well-proportioned body.

Jacqueline had also noticed Andrew immediately and she liked what she saw. She might have been a schoolgirl but she had the instincts of a woman and she knew full well when a boy was interested in her and responded accordingly.

Without any hesitation, she glided over to the side of the rink where Andrew was leaning. and they struck up a conversation. Andrew was almost too excited to speak. He could not quite believe that this glamorous figure was actually talking to him. They swapped pleasantries at first. What school do you go to? Who are your friends? That sort of thing.

Throughout this, Andrew was aware that she was sizing him up for romance. Her eyes kept panning up and down his body. It should have been the other way round but that was typical of Jacqueline. She had been pretty spoilt at home in south Wales. The only girl in a small family, she got what she wanted and knew full well how to manipulate people for her own advantage.

Andrew was the complete opposite. His mind was firmly focused on starting his own business one day and making a success of his life, almost to the exclusion of other, more social pleasures. Later he openly admitted he was completely swept off his feet by Jacqueline.

Jacqueline Morgan, jailed for two years for the grevious bodily harm of her husband.

Neither of them did much more skating that day. Instead, they wandered over to the coffee bar inside the ice rink and sat and chatted for what seemed like hours.

That evening, Andrew walked home from the rink on a romantic high. He had never before truly enjoyed the company of a girl. It was strange the way that just talking to Jacqueline had made him feel so happy.

After that first meeting, Andrew spent days trying to engineer a way to bump into Jacqueline again. He could not get her out of his mind. In the daytime he walked around in a virtual trance and at night he found it difficult to sleep. The only solution was to find her and ask her out properly.

Eventually his dream came true when he literally bumped into Jacqueline near her school in Cardiff. Andrew was the happiest man in the world when he spotted her and he immediately picked up where they had left off at the ice rink.

Jacqueline was flattered by Andrew's interest and liked the fact that he was a couple of years older than her. She always found the boys at school a little immature for her liking. Then there was the added bonus that Andrew was starting to make his own living, so he always had more cash to spend than the boys at school. All these factors were important to Jacqueline. She only wanted — and often got — the best. She was used to being treated like a little princess at home, so she expected the same from her boyfriends.

Over the following year, Andrew and Jacqueline dated on a very regular basis. Andrew's infatuation with his young girlfriend developed into a full-blown romance and they enjoyed going to the cinema, eating out and sometimes making love.

When Jacqueline announced she was leaving school, Andrew did not hesitate to suggest they should move in together. He could think of nothing better than waking up with his beautiful girlfriend beside him every morning. He would he the envy of his friends because they were always reminding him what a good catch he had made in Jacqueline.

So, just before her seventeenth birthday, Andrew and Jacqueline moved in together. On the surface it seemed like a match made in heaven. With her stunning blonde hair and bubbly personality, Jacqueline was capable of being a great laugh. She could even drink most of Andrew's friends under the table.

However, there was one aspect of Jacqueline's character that Andrew only discovered after they had moved in together. She had a really nasty temper. The slightest thing would set her off. Something as unimportant as spilling tea on her dress before going off to work would do it and Andrew learnt to shrink into the background whenever she had such tantrums.

One time, Jacqueline flipped out about a girl who she claimed was eyeing Andrew up when they went out to the pub with some pals. Andrew had noticed how Jacqueline became really quiet about halfway through the evening but thought nothing of it until they got home. Then she had gone completely crazy with him, shouting and swearing about 'that bitch' and how she had spotted Andrew smiling back at the other girl.

Andrew was bemused and slightly disturbed by Jacqueline's outburst and told her not to be so ridiculous, but that just made Jacqueline worse. She continued ranting and raving at him and then made an extraordinary admission.

'I've hit girls before and if she comes near you I'll get her.'

Andrew sat in stunned silence for a few moments, trying to digest what his lover was saying. Then Jacqueline proudly elaborated. It transpired that she had once broken a girl's jaw at school when that girl dared to flirt with one of her boyfriends before Andrew. Jacqueline then went on to reveal that there had been other times, too. In fact, she seemed to have made quite a habit of beating people up during her school years.

With a shake of her long, curly, blonde hair she turned towards Andrew as if to say, 'Don't mess with me.' At least that's what Andrew thought many years later, although he then had no inkling of what was eventually going to happen. In his mind, Jacqueline was the girl of his dreams, the girl he loved and adored and the person he wanted to spend the rest of his life with.

For two years the couple lived reasonably happily together. There was the occasional temper tantrum from Jacqueline but they always kissed and made up. Andrew acknowledged that no one was perfect, so putting up with a fiery lady did not seem so bad. In any case, there were other advantages.

Andrew loved being out with Jacqueline because she stood out in a crowd because of her penchant for wonderfully tight-fitting mini-dresses and figure-enhancing stilettos. He knew that most of his friends were still really jealous of the way he had hooked up with such a good-looking girl and Jacqueline revelled in all the attention.

She was particularly pleased with the way that Andrew had started his own business installing satellite TV systems and was building it up into a highly profitable operation. Her parents had always told her to make sure that the man in her life was a good wage earner, so Andrew fitted the bill perfectly.

Jacqueline accidentally got pregnant two years later but there was no remorse at the news. The couple were financially stable so it would have happened eventually anyway. Andrew was particularly delighted because he thought a child was just what Jacqueline needed. He secretly believed that the responsibility of parenthood might just calm down her vicious temper and that that would be a very good thing indeed.

When a little boy — Rhys — was born, both Andrew and Jacqueline saw him as the final seal on their relationship. Naturally she adored the child and seemed to take to motherhood like a duck to water.

Andrew could not quite believe his good fortune in having such a wonderful girl as Jacqueline as his partner. Now that they had Rhys there was only one more thing to make the perfect picture complete. Both sets of parents had started to remind Andrew and Jacqueline that they really should get married, especially as their relationship seemed so solid. Jacqueline appeared the more reluctant of the two actually to commit to wedlock but Andrew interpreted this as the response of a thoroughly modem woman brought up in the 1990s where a marriage certificate is of no real significance.

Eventually, Jacqueline did bow to parental pressure. When Rhys was three years old, the couple married in a quiet ceremony near their home. Immediately after the wedding, however, things started to change.

Jacqueline became much moodier than she had been previously. She seemed dissatisfied with her life at home looking after Rhys while Andrew worked long hours to keep his business up and running. Then there was that temper of hers. It seemed as if the slightest thing could set her off and once Andrew caught a glimpse of that fury in her sea-blue eyes, it was a danger signal of what was to come. Usually, he would just leave the room or change the subject. There was absolutely no point in prolonging the agony.

In many ways, Andrew tried to bury his head in his work and not worry too much about Jacqueline's mood swings. He just hoped it would all blow over. At home, however, Jacqueline was getting more and more depressed. She talked to her other girlfriends about their lives and discovered they were all going out to nightclubs and having a good time while she was stuck at home with Rhys. Jacqueline was a fun girl at heart and she did not like the fact that other people were having a more enjoyable time than her. Being married made it worse because Jacqueline felt as if there would never be an escape from the drudgery and boredom. She had signed away her rights to freedom and she did not like it one little bit.

'I want more freedom. I'm going to move out.

Andrew couldn't quite believe his ears when Jacqueline announced her plans minutes after he came home from work one night. He never thought it would come to this but, as had always been the case between them, he could not stand in her way. Something stopped him from trying too hard to persuade her not to go. It was a feeling he had. He did not want the marriage to end but he feared that unless she got her wish, something terrible might happen.

On the surface he pleaded with Jacqueline to stay but he knew all along that her mind was made up. She told him she had spoken to her parents and they had agreed to let her and Rhys move in. It was for the best, she explained. Andrew wasn't entirely convinced but Jacqueline always got what Jacqueline wanted.

For the first few months of the split, Andrew and Jacqueline remained on reasonable terms. He would try to see Rhys as often as possible and she was genuinely pleased that his business was going from strength to strength.

The turning point came when Jacqueline heard on the grapevine that Andrew was seeing another girl. The fact that they had separated did not seem to matter to Jacqueline; she was still incensed that he was daring to go out with another woman right under her nose.

Andrew saw it slightly differently. He needed the company of another female and as Jacqueline had been the one who had insisted they separate, what was the harm in it?

When Andrew went to visit Rhys at Jacqueline's parents' home one day, he experienced a full-blown version of that vicious temper of hers. She screamed and yelled at him that she would not stand for him dating other women. He tried to reason with her but by that time she had turned into a wild, crazy, out-of-control personality and he could not handle it so he walked out.

A few days later, Jacqueline commenced divorce proceedings. Andrew was torn between sadness at the break-up of his family and the relief he felt because that temper of Jacqueline's really did worry him.

Then a strange thing happened because Jacqueline became more like her old self again. It was almost as if the divorce proceedings had lifted a veil of insecurity from over her head. She became much more friendly towards Andrew and he became very confused. Only a few weeks earlier his estranged wife had been attacking him like a lunatic. Now she was giving him long lingering kisses every time he popped round to see Rhys.

Behind Jacqueline's charm, however, there was an ulterior motive. She mentioned to Andrew that she wanted him to sell their family house and all their possessions so that she could have her share. Andrew agreed but said that it would have to wait until the divorce was finalised.

The next thing he knew, Jacqueline was on his doorstep with Rhys, announcing that they were moving back in. For a few moments Andrew thought that perhaps they were going to give the marriage another go, but Jacqueline soon put paid to that notion.

Within minutes of arriving at the house she made it very clear to him that she had not come back for any romantic reasons; she simply wanted to stake a claim on the house and their possessions. Andrew finally conceded to friends that night that his marriage was well and truly over.

He soon started getting serious with his new girlfriend and promised himself he would try to end the marriage as cleanly and swiftly as possible so that both of them could get on with the rest of their lives. He also wanted to guarantee that little Rhys was not hurt.

However, having moved back into the house, Jacqueline now wanted Andrew to get out. She shouted and screamed at him on a regular basis, saying that he had no right to be there, but he had nowhere else to go. Every night it was the same old story. Andrew would come home exhausted from a hard day at work to face a barrage of abuse from his estranged wife. To start with, it was a generalised verbal attack that repeated over and over again that he had to get out. Then Jacqueline became more specific. 'I could have you done over for thirty quid.'

Andrew was staggered when he heard his wife's words. She couldn't possibly mean it, could she?

Then he looked at the cold, steely expression on her face and began to wonder. That night they hardly uttered another word to each other, but the damage had already been done.

A few weeks later, on 22 June 1993, Jacqueline picked up Rhys from a local child minder and arrived home at about five o'clock, almost exactly the same time as Andrew. The couple had agreed to take it in turns to look after their son and the plan that day was for Jacqueline to drop Rhys with Andrew, then go out with a friend and return home by nine that evening so that he could go out.

At about 8.45 p.m., having put Rhys to bed, Andrew had settled into a long comfortable hot bath when he heard Jacqueline come in.

In the hallway, she called out to the couple's dog and then, for some reason, locked him out in the back garden.

Just after that Andrew noticed that everything had gone deathly quiet. He gave it a few moments' thought then got out of the bath, put a towel round his waist and started to have a shave.

Suddenly the door burst open. Andrew just presumed it was Jacqueline or Rhys. Then he turned from the sink to face three men armed with baseball bats and crowbars.

The first man smashed Andrew clean across the face, then dropped his weapon and held him in a head lock. The two other men stood behind him as he yelled at them, 'Smash his right leg, smash his right leg, go for his knee.'

Andrew did not even think about the

significance of this remark until later when he realised that they must have known he had a steel plate in his right leg as a result of a serious car crash.

Too stunned even to be frightened, Andrew then suffered a series of hefty blows to the head and body. They were excruciatingly painful but then his body went completely numb, almost as if his entire internal system had shut down. Blood was pouring out of his wounds. Andrew did not even realise that half his skull had caved in as a result of one hefty baseball-bat blow to the side of his head. His brain had literally been punctured by the attackers and his body had basically 'slowed down' as a result.

Then, in the middle of all this, little Rhys woke up and started crying. In the background, Andrew just made out the sound of Jacqueline rushing up the stairs to come to his rescue. She burst into the room and pleaded with the attackers to stop but they took no notice.

The three men kept on smashing into Andrew for at least another three minutes before he collapsed on the bath-room floor, bloodied and beaten to a pulp. Relieved that it was all over and he was still just alive, Andrew managed to look up as they walked towards the door. One of the men took the crowbar he had used earlier and crashed it down on the left side of Andrew's rib cage. The pain was unbelievable and he kept smashing it down on Andrew over and over again before walking out of the house.

Despite the severe beating, Andrew never stopped worrying about his beloved Rhys and Jacqueline. He feared that they had been attacked by the intruders who had broken into his house and nearly killed him. God knows what they might have done to them.

A next-door neighbour called the emergency services after hearing the explosion of violence and minutes after the men had departed Andrew found himself being rushed to hospital in an ambulance with Jacqueline holding his hand and crying. It was a pitiful, heartbreaking scene.

At the hospital, doctors found that part of Andrew's skull had caved in, both his arms and legs were fractured and his spine and rib cage were seriously damaged. As he lay close to death in intensive care, medics also discovered that the blow to Andrew's head had caused a blood clot on the right side of his brain and he would need surgery to rebuild the right side of his head and face.

That same night, police and forensic experts swarmed all over the Morgan household in a bid to find clues as to the identity of his attackers.

Investigators swiftly tracked down a local boy who had seen the three men leaving the house and they identified the ringleader and the second man immediately. They were detained within hours. A warrant was issued for the arrest of the third man, who gave himself up the following day. Two days later, officers arrested Jacqueline on suspicion of being involved and took her to the police station to be questioned.

Back in hospital, Andrew Morgan was clinging to life following the brutal, apparently senseless, attack. Doctors gave strict instructions to his family that under no circumstances was he to be told of Jacqueline's involvement. There were genuine fears that if Andrew was told the truth it might 'send him over the edge'.

Then one of Andrew's friends visited the hospital and let slip to him that Jacqueline had set the whole thing up. Andrew was so shocked by the news that he instantly threw up over the side of the bed. He could not believe it. 'How could she have done that to me?' he kept thinking. How could she have let those thugs walk into their house armed with weapons when their child was sleeping nearby? Andrew knew that things had not exactly being going well between him and Jacqueline, but surely she could not do this?

As Andrew lay in that hospital bed, he

started to think back to those little tell-tale signs: the threat to get him beaten up for thirty pounds, the way the dog was locked out while he lay in the bath, the specific attack on his injured right leg. Then the police told him there were no signs of a forced entry, so how else could the men have got in?

A week after the attack, doctors decided it was safe to operate on Andrew. During ten hours of surgery they cut him from ear to ear over the top of his head, peeled back his face and inserted metal plates with nuts and bolts around his cheek, eye socket and skull.

By the time he was released from hospital, Jacqueline and the other men had been charged with wounding with intent to cause grievous bodily harm. Andrew took Rhys to live with his parents.

His life was destroyed. Before the attack he had a thriving business but now that had to be closed down. The following months were dreadful. Andrew could not sleep because he was so terrified he wouldn't wake up and when he did fall asleep he was plagued by horrendous nightmares.

At Cardiff Crown Court in January 1994, all three men admitted grievous bodily harm, but twenty-four-year-old Jacqueline denied the charge. In court she said she never intended Andrew to be harmed — just frightened.

The jury took just forty minutes to find her guilty but they convicted on a lesser count (which means no specific intent to injure was involved) because they couldn't prove she intended to hurt her husband so badly.

Andrew Morgan is trying to start his life again, but he is not fully recovered. When they caved in his skull, the bones crushed tendons in his eyes so he still has double vision and is due for further surgery. If that does not work, doctors have warned him to expect to suffer for the rest of his life.

'Jacqueline might look as pretty as a Barbie doll, but at the end of the day she's vicious. And I think that's the way she'll always be,' he said after the case.

Appetite for Murder

Rebecca Smith wrapped her arms around her sturdily-built lover and stroked the hairs on his chest. Then, with a sudden snake-like movement she snapped a hair out. He winced with pain, then saw the smile on her face and laughed. Rebecca did love to play games. She also loved to inflict a brief amount of pain on all around her — and that included her workman lover Thad.

Rebecca needed to be in control the whole time. The mother of three grown boys, she enjoyed the power to do whatever she wanted with Thad. Their passionate affair had reignited after a break of almost twenty years. The second time around, Thad later recalled, the love-making was even less inhibited.

Thad had first met Rebecca when she was married to the father of her three sons. She had told Thad that her husband was in the habit of beating her up. Within days of meeting, she lured him to her home on some pretext or other one afternoon and when she opened the front door with a silky dressing gown on, Thad knew they would end up in bed together.

That affair only lasted two months and mainly revolved around Rebecca's ability to enjoy sex in just about any place she happened to be at the moment the urge came upon her. Thad — then a young, impressionable teenager — was completely swept off his feet. She taught him things he never even knew existed.

Thad was heartbroken when Rebecca told him she was ending the relationship because she was moving out of state. Thad always reckoned that his disappointment about Rebecca's 'desertion' led him to marry and divorce four times before they met again.

In 1986, Thad ran into Rebecca in his local store in Laurinberg, North Carolina. She might have been twenty years older but she still cut a fine figure.

Rebecca was immediately entranced by Thad. He looked as magnificent as ever as she panned her eyes up and down his body while he stood there, slightly awkwardly talking to her. She decided there and then that she was going to have him again.

Just a few weeks later the affair restarted. The love-making was so wild and uninhibited that it was like starting a completely new relationship. As usual, Rebecca did most of the running. She would appear at Thad's little house on the edge of town whenever the moment took her fancy and Thad never failed to oblige. After those four disastrous marriages, this was the ideal relationship. He needed sex but the last thing he required was a full-time woman.

However, Thad soon began to discover that Rebecca's insatiable appetite for sex had developed in a quite unusual way since their earlier liaison. In fact, he started to wonder whether she wasn't just a little sick in the head because she did not seem to be able to enjoy traditional love making any more. There always had to be some dangerous edge to it.

Thad never forgot the time Rebecca showed

up at his house with her son Brian, then in his early twenties, and Brian's pretty young girlfriend. Thad was a little surprised as Rebecca usually demanded sex within minutes of arriving at Thad's house and he did not exactly expect her to bring guests, especially her own son.

The foursome enjoyed a few beers and some bourbon together and then, as her son and his girlfriend sat in the sitting room of the house, Rebecca stripped down to her stockings, bra and panties and did a little dance for her guests.

Both Brian and his girlfriend applauded and tried to encourage Rebecca to strip off completely. She did not need that much encouragement. Thad sat transfixed by the entire episode, unsure whether to applaud along with the others or to try to put a stop to the proceedings.

A few minutes later, Rebecca declared she was going to liven up the action even further. She told a stunned Thad that she wanted to go to the bedroom with him to have sex. Naturally, he obliged, although he couldn't help being a bit surprised that she talked that way in front of her own son.

Thad did not notice Rebecca winking at her son as she got up. A moment later she grabbed Thad's hand and pulled him towards the only bedroom in the house. Brian did the same with his girlfriend and followed his mother and her lover.

In the bedroom, Thad found himself even more confused. Rebecca calmly explained to her lover that she wanted her son to take photographs of them having sex. She said it almost as plainly as a mother might explain to her child that he should do his homework, although in this case it was obvious that Brian did not need teaching.

Brian's girlfriend giggled and then gave Brian the camera. Rebecca ripped open Thad's trousers and within minutes the flashbulb was popping over and over again ...

By the end of that evening, Thad felt rather differently about Rebecca. It was all very well enjoying outrageous sex in all sorts of weird and wonderful places but he did find it a bit strange to be performing in front of her son. It made him feel kind of uneasy.

When, a few weeks later, Rebecca added another unusual dimension to her illicit affair with Thad, he decided it was time to end the relationship.

The final straw came as Rebecca prepared to strip off for more sex as she sat on Thad's couch one afternoon. About to unhook her bra, she paused momentarily. 'Would you do me a big favour if I paid you five thousand dollars?' she asked, very matter-of-factly.

'What you want me to do for that kind of money?' replied a puzzled Thad.

'Kill Harold.'

There was a long silence as Thad considered why she should be asking him to kill her long-suffering husband Harold. The sex scene with her son had been weird enough but now the alarm bells were ringing continuously in his head.

'I don't go round killing people, Rebecca. It ain't right.'

'Oh well,' sighed Rebecca, still managing to make the entire conversation sound less important than if she was haggling over the price of a bag of apples at the local grocery store. 'Maybe you know someone else who'd do it.'

Thad was starting to get really uncomfortable now. 'Hell no. Just drop it, Rebecca.'

Rebecca finally got the message and changed the subject but Thad knew it was only a matter of time before she found herself an assassin.

Billy Ray McGee was the perfect replacement lover for Rebecca Smith after she and Thad finished their fling. Billy Ray was a fitness fanatic who'd become obsessed with weight training after a few stints in jail for thieving.

No one ever questioned Rebecca's motives in hooking up with Billy Ray. It was just taken for granted that she required abnormally large amounts of bedtime activity and that her husband Harold could never, in a month of Sundays, provide his wife with what she seemed to crave every moment of the day.

Harold was a quietly-spoken, shy type of guy. At the plant where he worked incredibly hard, he was well liked and renowned for working through lunch breaks and volunteering to do endless overtime.

Harold was so devoted to Rebecca that he even routinely handed over his entire pay packet to his wife, who gave him back thirty dollars a week spending money. He never once complained. He just wanted to ensure that she was constantly happy.

In July 1989, Harold excitedly told his work colleagues that he was looking forward to leaving his routine world for a fishing trip. Fishing was a pleasure Harold usually enjoyed with his three stepsons. On this occasion, however, he was going alone because all of the boys — Rebecca's children by her previous marriage — were employed full time and could not get any time off to join him.

'He was so happy,' explained one co-worker at the plant. 'All he talked about was going to the beach and catching twenty-three fish at a time.'

Harold had worked at the Corning plant since 1973 and had built his earnings up to a very impressive twenty-two thousand dollars a year, considerably more than his base salary because he was so willing to work overtime.

Since his marriage to Rebecca more than fifteen years earlier, Harold had always got on very well with his three stepsons and, besides fishing trips, they often went on vacations in the mountains and lakes nearby. Harold had, according to relatives, 'raised those boys as if they were his own flesh and blood'.

On the face of it, Harold's marriage to Rebecca seemed perfectly normal but, inevitably, he began to hear some of the rumours about his wife's recreational habits and even confessed to one colleague at work that everything was not going so well on the domestic front.

However, Harold had insisted that he would sort out his 'problems' in his own careful way. Undoubtedly, he knew that those 'problems' had been caused by his wife's interest in other, younger men. Whether he actually chose never to confront his wife about her addiction to sex no one knows, but he certainly did not want to face up to the facts.

There was another very strange aspect to his marriage which was not so apparent — Rebecca's obsession with black magic. In early 1989, Rebecca started visiting a local woman who claimed to be a witch capable of casting spells and putting hexes on people. Rebecca was particularly interested in cursing her husband's life. She complained bitterly that Harold was no fun and that she was completely bored by her life as Mrs Smith.

Still, none of this was going to ruin Harold's plans for a quiet fishing trip where he could escape all the pressures of life and just worry about how many nibbles he was going to get on the end of his line.

On Friday, 13 July 1989, Harold set off in his blue Chevrolet truck for the two-hour drive to the family's holiday trailer at Cherry Grove, a beautiful strip of coastline on South Carolina's Grand Strand, which stretches some forty miles between Georgetown and Little River.

On that Sunday (15 July), with Harold safely packed off on his getaway break at the trailer, Rebecca Smith enjoyed an afternoon of love making with Billy Ray before he took a nap. She awoke him early that evening and they smoked a cannabis joint and snorted cocaine before she announced that she wanted to take her son Brian Locklear to the beach so that he could go fishing with Harold.

Accompanying Rebecca and Brian on the drive were Billy Ray McGee and a relative,

Charles Gainey. The four of them took the car of another of Rebecca's sons who was working at the time. Brian drove and the foursome got a little spooked when they hit a wild animal on the road to the beach.

'I knew something bad was going to happen after that,' explained Gainey later.

When the foursome arrived at the beach area, they stopped for a short time at a picturesque fishing pier to admire the sunset and then drove to the mobile-home park where the Smith family trailer was located.

Gainey was puzzled when Rebecca barked orders at her son to dim the car lights as he drove towards the trailer, and then she instructed him not to park near the actual trailer.

'You and Billy lie down on the floor. I don't want Harold knowing I got a lot of company,' muttered Rebecca coldly. They did as they were told.

Moments later Rebecca and her beloved son disappeared in the direction of the trailer. Suddenly, a light came on in the trailer and they watched as Harold came to the door to let them in. Gainey stayed out of view but later claimed he was puzzled by the fact that Rebecca was hiding a baseball bat behind her back at the moment her husband opened the door.

For a few more minutes Gainey and Billy Ray remained hidden in the back of the car. Then Brian appeared and ordered them to go back to the pier and get some soft drinks. Gainey and Billy Ray returned within ten minutes to be greeted by an excited Rebecca, who rushed to the car and said, 'I did it. I did it. He's dead.'

All three of them entered the trailer. Gainey was ordered to go down the hall and 'look at what Becky had done'. Harold was lying half out of bed, half on the floor, making gurgling noises. Just at that moment, one of the men — they disputed who in later testimony — took the baseball bat off a counter and smashed Harold in the head again 'to finish him off'.

Then Gainey watched in astonishment as Brian Locklear grabbed some hand lotion from a nearby cupboard and smothered it all over his dead stepfather's fingers so that he could remove a horseshoe-shaped ring. Meanwhile, a cool-as-ice Rebecca Smith was moving around the trailer wiping things down with a cloth so that there would be no fingerprints on display when the police arrived at the scene.

As they were leaving, McGee — the only professional crimmal among them — smashed the flimsy door to the trailer with the baseball bat just to ensure that the entire incident looked as if it had happened following a break-in.

During the drive home they pulled the car up on a bridge and Rebecca's son Brian tossed the bloodied baseball bat into the river.

After returning to the family home in Laurinberg a few hours later, Rebecca ordered Brian to take the horseshoe ring to the witch doctor she had previously visited. She told him it was 'payment' for her previous efforts to kill Harold by means of witchcraft before she decided upon a more traditional approach.

After visiting the witch doctor, Brian returned to the family home to fetch a pair of Harold's trousers. They put these in a cake pan along with some sulphur and red onions, then burned the whole lot. The witch doctor had assured them that this would prevent the police from tracking down Rebecca and her fellow killers.

With the killing completed, Rebecca decided that the next stage of her plan should be put into operation.

'You gotta help. It's my husband. I'm real worried about him.' Rebecca Smith sounded very concerned about her husband's whereabouts when she called the North Myrtle Beach police department in South Carolina. She told the operator she had been unable to get her husband on the phone despite repeated attempts. She was afraid something might have happened to him.

Communications technician Dot Sorra assured her that just as soon as the police information computer network was programmed, the information would be acted upon.

Patrolman Asa Bailey took the call from a dispatcher and headed up to the trailer park at Cherry Grove. At first he got no answer after knocking on the door. He walked around and peered through the windows, but everything seemed okay.

Then he got round to the back door. Again, there was no answer but still nothing seemed amiss. Back at the front door a few minutes later, Bailey noticed the doorknob was scraped and dented with what appeared to be pry marks. He tried the door properly this time. It was unlocked.

Bailey opened the door tentatively, then called out as he walked into the trailer's small living area. Next to it was a clean, compact kitchen with hardly an item out of place. Bailey stood and considered the scene for a few moments. If someone had battered and smashed their way in, surely things would be in a more chaotic state?

Then Bailey walked down the narrow hallway towards the only bedroom on the left. He glanced through the door and did a double take.

Lying half on and half off a blood-stained bed was the body of a man dressed only in under-pants. Bailey could only see the back of the dead man's head, lying in a large bloody stain on the carpet.

After rapidly searching the rest of the mobile home in case anyone else was present, Bailey returned to his police cruiser and made an urgent request for a supervisor and a detective.

Shortly after 2 p.m., Chief of Detectives Walt Floyd and Detective Don Repec were making a detailed inspection of the crime scene. At first they could not even find anything to provide identification of the victim although there were many bloodstains in the bedroom. Large quantities also blotted the bedclothing and the floor under the victim's head. Blood was also splattered over the wall and even on the shade of the bedside lamp. Floyd and Repec immediately deduced that the drops of blood must have been shed in the backswing of a bloody weapon.

Detective Repec painstakingly photographed every angle of the death scene with a video camera as his colleagues began their meticulous search of the premises.

It was only when the victim's body was moved and turned over that it became obvious just how horrific a beating had been inflicted on Harold Smith. The battering had been so severe that one eye socket had been crushed and the eyeball itself knocked out of the victim's head.

Both detectives were concerned by the lack of evidence of any furniture or belongings being disturbed and they rapidly established that the entire trailer had been cleaned of fingerprints. The North Myrtle Beach police force had not dealt with a murder inquiry for four years so this investi-gation was getting the full treatment.

A few hours into their inquiries one of the investigators discovered that someone had used the toilet in the trailer but had not flushed it. Probers took samples of the urine still in the toilet bowl and, a few days later, it was determined that the sample contained cocaine residue. The victim had no known involvement with drugs and there was no evidence of drug taking in his body.

The discovery of that cocaine convinced the two detectives that they were dealing with something much more complex than a straightforward burglary that had turned to violence. They rapidly established that Rebecca Smith had a vast sexual appetite and some of her conquests began, as they sometimes say, to sing like canaries.

On 8 August 1989, Rebecca Smith and Billy Ray McGee were arrested and charged with the murder of Harold Dean Smith. Her relative,

Charles Gainey, was charged as an accessory, as was Brian Locklear, despite the damning evidence against him.

With information provided by Gainey, lawmen located a baseball bat that had been tossed off a bridge over the nearby Waccamaw River. The State Law Enforcement Division (SLED) analysts detected bloodstains on the object. They also discovered, embedded on the bat's grain, paint that was later matched to paint on the door at the murder scene.

Shortly after her arrest, Rebecca Smith made a statement to police in which she blamed Billy Ray McGee for the murder of her husband. She claimed that he was the one who actually smashed her husband to death with that baseball bat.

Then her loyal son Brian also claimed that McGee was the actual killer. Meanwhile McGee claimed that Rebecca Smith had persuaded him to help her with the killing after she regularly visited him in jail during an earlier sentence, each time bringing his spending money in amounts of $15 to $30. Rebecca even bought cocaine through McGee on his release and he accompanied her on at least twenty visits to a witch doctor whom Smith wanted to put a death spell on her husband.

In early 1990, all four suspects — Billy McGee, Rebecca Smith, Charles Gainey and Brian Locklear

— were indicted on various charges in connection with the murder of Harold Smith.

In December 1990, almost eighteen months after her husband's murder, Rebecca Smith went on trial for her life in the Horry County Courthouse in Conway. The other three had already entered pleas In connection with the case.

The jury deliberated for nine hours before returning a guilty verdict and Rebecca Smith was sentenced to die in the electric chair. However, the case was appealed and at a retrial in February 1994, Rebecca Smith was again found guilty of first-degree murder but the jury declined to give her the death penalty. She was sentenced to life imprisonment and is currently serving her term in the South Carolina correction system. The new trial was further complicated by fresh claims from her son Brian that he was the one who had beaten and killed Harold Smith. This evidence was discounted after the court was told that Brian Locklear was a self-confessed bisexual who had tested HIV-positive.

Meanwhile, Billy McGee and Brian Locklear were sentenced to thirty-five-year jail terms and Gainey got fifteen years, but was released on parole after helping authorities with evidence against Rebecca Smith.

The Politics of Revenge

Judge's wife Valerie Harkess and her two attractive married daughters were filled with dread the day they discovered that one-time British MP and Tory minister Alan Clark was planning to publish his memoirs. For all three had, at one time, been seduced by the millionaire politician and they feared that their reputations would be irreparably damaged if he revealed any details about the sex romps all of them had experienced with Clark, a self-confessed lothario.

As the publication date of Clark's tell-all diaries rapidly approached, Valerie consoled and comforted her younger daughter Josephine, aged thirty-four, who was particularly distraught at the prospect of having her name publicised. Valerie's other daughter Alison had married and settled down in a different corner of the world and wanted nothing to do with the entire scenario.

Valerie and Josephine feared Old Etonian Clark was going to make references to his sexual liaisons with all three, describing them proudly as sex games ... and not obliquely enough to conceal the Harkess family name.

Valerie even contacted Clark and asked him if the autobiography made any mention of her and her daughters. The one-time minister assured her that they were not mentioned by name.

When Valerie picked up a copy of the book as soon as it was published in her new home in South Africa, she was outraged. He had jokingly referred to a mother and daughter as his 'coven'. Valerie and her daughter felt betrayed. Valerie might be now enjoying a very privileged lifestyle in a fortified, white, gabled house called Raphael in Constantia, one of Cape Town's most prosperous suburbs, but that did not make it any easier to handle.

It was then that Valerie and Josephine decided to initiate one of the most extraordinary examples of female revenge ever witnessed in Britain. Rather than face an embarrassing whispering campaign, they revealed the full sordid details of their bedtime exploits with Clark to Britain's raciest, most-read tabloid newspaper, the News of the World.

In a remarkable cloak-and-dagger operation, News of the World journalists flew secretly to the Harkess home in South Africa where they were told an extraordinary account of sexual promiscuity at the very top of the Tory party. Valerie Harkess told the paper: 'Man has virtually ruined all our lives, mine, my husband's and my two daughters'. He is a depraved animal.'

So it was with these words that Valerie and Josephine Harkess launched their bitter battle to expose casanova Alan Clark as one of the most notorious womanisers seen in British politics this century. They claimed they had endured years of sordid sex with the kinky former MP. Among the tamer claims against millionaire Clark was that he used Valerie for afternoon sex sessions in his flat near the House of Commons, and that he seduced Josephine's sister Mison when she was going through a particularly difficult time in her life.

Clark was also accused of taking advantage of Valerie's other daughter Josephine after she had been to see Clark to ask for his help. Other assorted claims were also made against Clark by the women. It all added up to a very sordid package for the News of the World.

Married Clark allegedly worked his way through the Harkess family during a fourteen-year affair with Valerie. By deciding to reveal the truth about the smutty one-time cabinet member, Valerie found herself having to confess her adultery to her husband James.

For some reason, her husband decided not to leave his cheating wife. She explained in breathless tones: 'I'd feared James might take it badly and leave us, but he's a wonderful, tolerant and forgiving Christian man. Our marriage is intact. I know it will take years for us to build the trust up again but we intend to do it.

'I expect no sympathy for my actions, nor for those of my daughters, but had it not been for these foul diaries, I might have taken the secret of my affair with Alan to my grave.

Valerie and her daughter continued on the warpath against Clark by flying into London from South Africa to disclose more of the former politician's most sensitive secrets. Those included a series of letters and cards which gave an astonishing insight into the mind of the man who became one of Margaret Thatcher's most trusted confidants.

The Harkess family had already employed the services of one Max Clifford, a renowned publicist without whom no tawdry political scandal was complete in the 1990s. Just hours before the family flew into London's Heathrow Airport, Clifford proudly announced: 'The circus is coming into town.' Valerie and her clan were not going to let the matter just fizzle out. She and her husband talked about confronting Clark.

The News of the World's decision to splash the women's extraordinary story across many pages of their edition on Sunday, 29 May 1994, was just the tip of the iceberg. Within days, the Harkess women were accused of being 'below-stairs types' by Clark's proud wife Jane, responding to reporters questions outside the family's vast castle in Kent. However, Valerie and Josephine came back with a vengeance.

Valerie, at fifty-six still a very attractive woman, decided to exact every last drop of revenge by giving an even more detailed account of her fourteen-year affair with Clark to The Sun newspaper on 1 June 1994. She disclosed how she first met Clark when she was an eighteen-year-old law student and how he made a pass at her when he dined with her and her then husband at London's upmarket Grosvenor House Hotel. Valerie even told how Clark ingratiated himself into her family to such a degree that her own husband encouraged her to go out for lunch with the Tory MP.

Eventually, she gave in to his demands and made love with Clark in his brother's house in London. Twisting the knife of revenge as sharply as she could, Valerie revealed: 'He was a very straight lover, but he was very selfish. He was only interested in his own satisfaction and he didn't bother with foreplay.'

The affair continued for another ten years, on and off, until Valerie visited London from her family's new home in South Africa and discovered that her elder daughter Alison was sleeping with Clark.

'I felt physically sick, and full of blame for my daughter being seduced,' she informed the world.

Yet, despite her disgust at discovering that her daughter was sleeping with her illicit lover, Valerie continued having sex sessions with Clark.

In 1983 — with Clark now firmly entrenched as a junior minister and one of Margaret Thatcher's most trusted advisers — he invited his secret married lover out for dinner with her other daughter Josephine. Then, in front of Clark, Josephine broke down and confessed that she, too, had been having an affair with Clark.

'The pain was so bad that if Jo hadn't been there I might have killed him with my bare hands,' insisted Valerie years later.

Despite her outrage, Valerie admitted that she continued to be addicted to Clark — and a year later she went to bed with him again.

'He dismissed what had happened as if it had just been a natural progression. I felt I was an adulterous wife, a bad mother and a worthless person. I was almost beyond caring what I thought of myself any more and blindly I slept with him a few more times almost like a zombie.'

Finally, in the late eighties, Valerie started to see the light as far as Alan Clark was concerned. In wonderfully explicit terms she explained: 'I realised for the first time what rotten teeth he had. They were like nasty pebbles and his face showed a shifty, ageing man kidding himself he was attractive to women.

'This shrivelled husk then had the nerve to suggest we went to bed once more. I said no, and walked out of his life.'

With a final swipe at her onetime bed partner, Valerie added: 'I hate Alan Clark for ever being born.'

Next it was Josephine's turn to exact her revenge upon the bed-hopping Tory. She claimed Clark had seduced her when was in a drunken stupor and insisted he took advantage of her when she turned to him for support as she battled alcohol addiction.

'I turned to Alan for comfort — he was Mother's friend, he had known me since I was a child. What I got were a few minutes of sex, sex I cannot even remember because of the condition I was in. I can remember feeling dirty. He made me feel like a dog.'

Despite her earlier 'disgust', the following night Josephine slept with Clark again. However, Clark was a bitter disappointment, which was much the same emotion her mother had felt after her first few sexual encounters with him.

Sticking the knife firmly into Clark, Josephine uttered the damning words: 'He seduced me when I was at my most vulnerable and when he knew I had no defences. That is something I cannot forgive him for. Alan obviously thought that because of his power, money and position he could expose us to ridicule and get away with it. Well he bloody well can't.'

Even Valerie's long–suffering husband, former Judge James Harkess, got in on the act by insisting: 'Valerie and I are more than just husband and wife. We are best friends, too, and nothing can destroy that. Certainly not a sick and sexually depraved man like Alan Clark.'

Just to make his point absolutely clearly to the world, Mr Harkess posed for The Sun newspaper with a horsewhip in one hand and a promise to use it on Alan Clark if he had the opportunity.

Alan Clark even managed to embroil his own long-suffering wife Jane in the scandal when she swiftly launched a loyal counter–attack. Breaking off from feeding the chickens at the couple's Saltwood Castle home, she told reporters that hints from the Harkess women that Clark had offered to buy their silence were absolutely not true.

'I was so cross when I heard that's what they were saying that I had to come straight down here and tell you the truth.' Mrs Clark said that, despite her husband's numerous confessions of infidelity, she still stood by him. It was an astonishing statement when one considers that she married him when she was just sixteen (he was thirty) and had somehow survived almost forty years of his philandering. She even told one friend a few days later that she considered his other women as 'bluebottles' whom she would like to crush.

Clark himself rounded off the entire circus by admitting he deserved a horsewhipping. 'It's a bit old–fashioned, but I suppose what I did deserves it.'

Sugar Daddy

Former magistrate Graham Partridge still had a keen eye for the ladies, even though he was pushing seventy-five years of age. Long since parted from his invalid wife, he simply thrived in the company of women, most of whom were at least forty years his junior. To Graham Partridge, the female members of the species were there to honour and obey him, especially when it came to the bedroom.

It was hardly surprising, therefore, when Graham's attention was caught by a familiar-looking woman waiting on the corner of the street near her home in the west Wales town of Llangoedmor. As his eyes panned up and down her rather shapely body, he realised that she was an attractive redhead whom he used to see going into her ballet school opposite his office years previously. Graham Partridge never forgot a pretty face. This was too good an opportunity for Graham to pass up. He stopped his car, rolled down the window and offered the woman a lift.

Kathryn George-Harries was flattered by the old man's attention and readily accepted. She later realised that when she got into his car that morning, she somehow instantly knew that they were about to embark on a relationship.

Kathryn was already vaguely acquainted with Graham through her family's business dealings with the ex-IP. He was a highly respected member of the small, rural community in which they both lived. Twice Graham had even stood as Conservative parliamentary candidate for the area.

At twenty-five, and considering that she was in the middle of training to be a solicitor, Kathryn happened to be a very vulnerable, unworldly woman. Perhaps that was what attracted Graham Partridge to her. He could mould her into whatever he wanted her to be, whenever he wanted. She had a kind of sensitivity which he immediately decided to capitalise on.

Kathryn was entranced by Graham as they drove together that morning. She did not realise he was so old and thought he was in his early sixties. In any case, he had the looks of a younger man and a sparkle in his eye which tantalised her from the moment they met.

Within weeks, Graham and Kathryn were enjoying a tempestuous sexual relationship conducted in absolute secrecy. He had insisted that no one knew about their affair because of their families' links and she had accepted his condition because it seemed reasonable considering there was such a vast age gap between them.

Love-making was remarkably energetic and adventurous considering his age. Graham even revealed later that, before making love, Kathryn liked to tantalise him by caressing the long barrels of his collection of guns. She also really enjoyed lifting her skirt up to reveal 'legs that went on for ever'. He also claimed that she was always the one who begged him to have sex with her. Graham assured one friend that Kathryn was definitely GIB — good in bed.

However, after a few months of their twice-weekly romps at Graham's £500,000 farmhouse in nearby Carmarthen, Kathryn began to feel the strain of their constant ducking and diving to avoid the gossips of the village, many of whom were already well aware of Graham's fondness for young ladies.

She also felt constantly guilty about the relationship. She hated the fact that she was abusing her family's trust by hiding the truth from them. Kathryn had a secret life that she could not discuss with anyone and it was putting enormous strain on her.

Then there was all the juggling that had to be performed. They could never be seen out together in the area, so candle-lit, romantic meals in local restaurants were out of the question. Most times their 'romance' involved Kathryn sneaking into Graham's home and sharing a bottle of his vintage wine, followed by a rapid ascent to the master bedroom.

In many ways it was an insidious process. Gradually, it became as regular as clockwork and although Kathryn was well aware of the pointless nature of it all, she simply could not stop herself. Each time she tried to question the wisdom of conducting a clandestine affair with a man old enough to be her grandfather, she would find herself sucked back into his sexual web of complicity.

Kathryn knew she needed help and advice but she was up against an emotional brick wall. She couldn't discuss it with anyone because then she would be betraying his trust. As the months turned into a year, Kathryn realised that she had gone beyond breaking point and back again. It was like a huge vicious, never-ending sexual circle.

After about eighteen months, her affair with Graham became such a strain that she suffered regular bouts of exhaustion and was drained of all enthusiasm for anything other than those twice-weekly sex sessions at his house. Her judgement began to be impaired. She began to feel seething jealousy whenever she found any hint of other girlfriends at the house.

At first, she did not say anything to Graham but, as her suspicions grew, so did her complete and utter insecurity about their relationship. Although she knew full well that it could never end in marriage. she wanted to be his only woman. She wanted to prove to Graham Partridge that she was capable of being everything to him: lover, girlfriend, helper, friend.

However, Graham wasn't looking for anything other than an occasional bed partner and he preferred to have a few of those on tap at any one time to satisfy his sexual appetite and general lust for life. As he told one friend: 'I prefer the company of women after 6 p.m.' In other words, females were his staple diet. As long as he had the urge to make love, he wanted a whole harem in close proximity.

Sometimes Graham would drop hints to Kathryn which suggested she was over-awed by her older lover. Nothing could have been further from the truth. She was a well-qualified woman in the middle of studying for a professional career, not a square-bottomed peasant or one of the chiffon-clad darlings who she suspected were among the regular visitors to the Partridge bedroom when she was not around.

As Kathryn later explained: 'I come from a middle-class family and have never been impressed by wealth. In any case, he wasn't half as wealthy as people thought.'

Kathryn also later insisted that she never actually loved Graham Partridge although she was certainly growing completely obsessed with him. Part of that obsession was an ever-increasing expectancy that he should be faithful to her.

For his part, Graham was not particularly bothered. He sensed that she was getting too possessive and wanted to end the relationship nicely and calmly if she continued her obsessive behaviour. He believed that she was expecting too much from him. He feared she might want to move in with him and that was definitely not what Graham Partridge wanted. In his eyes that was crossing the border of what any relationship meant to him. He actually believed that having sex twice a week with a woman almost fifty years his junior was nothing more than a 'laid-back friendship'. For all his experience with women, Graham did not really understand or appreciate them.

On the evening of 9 May 1990, Kathryn called at Graham's farmhouse, expecting, naturally, to end up in his bedroom. Graham was not in so she decided to wait for him to return, presuming that they would, as usual, sleep together that night.

Then she heard a car coming up the driveway. As it approached she saw that Graham was being driven by another lady friend of his, called Patricia Plewes. When he saw Kathryn waiting for him, Graham immediately sensed trouble. 'Oh my God, there goes my good night's sleep,' he thought. Typically charming, even in the face of such adversity, Graham invited both women into his house for a nightcap. That was his first mistake of the evening.

Within minutes of settling in the kitchen with a glass of wine each, Kathryn exploded. 'You're sleeping with him,' she accused Patricia Plewes.

Graham was appalled by what he heard and immediately insisted that Kathryn should leave the house. Then he considered the situation and realised that she would simply hang around outside until he let her in, so he asked Patricia to take him back to his friend's house where he had been earlier that night.

Kathryn was horrified. How could he be interested in such a ghastly woman? How could he betray their relationship so brazenly? How could he humiliate her in such a cruel manner?

Graham Partridge knew full well that Kathryn was about to 'blow her lid' at any moment. He got up. 'I'll be back in a while,' he told Kathryn before leaving the farmhouse with Patricia.

Kathryn never once questioned the honesty of

the last words he uttered to her. She fully expected him to return to her so that they could retire to bed and reignite their passion for one another. She sat at the table of his vast kitchen and started counting the minutes. After half an hour, she decided to open a bottle of his best wine from the vast collection in the cellar.

Three hours later, Kathryn staggered to the phone on the kitchen wall and dialled the home of the woman who had driven off with Graham. When Patricia Plewes picked up the phone, Kathryn exploded with jealous rage and demanded that Graham Partridge come back immediately. 'Send Graham home. I'm tart number one,' Kathryn screamed at her rival before slamming the phone down.

By this time, Kathryn's mind was a scrambled mess of emotional turmoil. She kept thinking that what had happened with the other woman meant that she was nothing more than one of his many bits on the side. For the first time it was dawning on her that she meant very little to him. The hurt was overwhelming.

Kathryn now realised that material possessions were far more important to Graham Partridge than people. She looked around at all the valuable antiques in the house and decided that the best way to hurt him was to destroy his belongings. If she destroyed them, then she could destroy all the pain and hurt. Kathryn had been pushed around for too long. She was going to smash everything to pieces.

She started with the clothes in his wardrobes. That would punish the always dapper and immaculately turned-out Graham Partridge. Then her attention was drawn to the four-poster bed where she and Graham had made hot, passionate love so often. It had to be destroyed because it represented the very epicentre of their relationship. She jumped up and down on it more ferociously than during any of their love-making efforts. She pulled at the bedhead until it ripped away then went back to jumping until the base snapped and the bed sagged. Then she staggered drunkenly back to the kitchen, took all the eggs from the fridge and smeared them over the walls.

Next she started systematically smashing every window in the house. Then she headed for the antiques in the drawing room. She was on a roller-coaster ride of drunken revenge and nothing was going to stop her. Brandishing a screwdriver and knife she slashed at the sofas and then waded into his finest china which stood sedately in a special display cupboard.

Kathryn just did not care any more. She had got to the point of no return.

After an hour and a half of non-stop destruction, in which she had injured herself quite seriously with all that flying glass and crockery, Kathryn stopped, satisfied that sufficient damage had been done to the man who had hurt her so badly. Only the cat and her china food bowl escaped Kathryn's violence.

When it was over she felt elated. She knew full well what the consequences of her actions would be but she didn't care. This was the best feeling in the world. He had got everything he deserved.

Kathryn was covered in blood and feathers but feeling absolutely wonderful, even liberated. She had exorcised everything that had happened to her during that two-year relationship.

She scrunched out of the house through piles of broken Doulton china and a sea of smashed glass with a look of sheer and complete satisfaction at a job well done. She had got to the end of her tether and dealt with her problem by causing £18,000 worth of damage to the property.

As the effects of the wine began to wear off, Kathryn did wonder how she had managed to cause so much destruction, but she never once felt any regret for her actions. She knew that if she had not done it then she would have continued seething about him for the rest of her life.

Next morning, Kathryn awoke, still in a partial drunken stupor. She heard the noise of someone smashing open the door that she had double-locked before collapsing in one of the spare bedrooms in the early hours. Kathryn realised it had to be the police and, for ten long seconds, considered climbing out of the window and making her escape. She knew that her life was about to undergo the most incredible, radical change but she felt strangely at peace with herself. Later, she compared it to the feeling of a condemned man on death row.

She stumbled out on to the landing to be greeted by two police officers. Graham Partridge was standing sheepishly behind them. She knew — they all knew. No explanation was necessary.

'I am not mad. I am not mad. I am not mad.' She repeated the words over and over again. Kathryn was well aware that she was guilty and would go to jail for what she had done but she had been perfectly content to wait for the cavalry to turn up and arrest her.

When she got to the police station a short time later, she even went through the charge sheet systematically ticking off the items she had destroyed. The police recalled her as being remarkably business-like about the entire incident.

At Swansea Crown Court, in January 1991, Kathryn pleaded guilty to a charge of criminal damage, and the following March she was sentenced. 'There were gasps in the court but I was expecting it,' she later recalled.

Kathryn was sentenced to six months in jail but was released after three months for good behaviour. Recorder David Hale said that she had been guilty of wanton destruction and had jeopardised her career as a lawyer. 'You have a volatile nature. What you did that night cannot be unpunished or overlooked. There is some truth in the psychiatrists' opinion that you derived some gratification from your notoriety. It shows your complete lack of remorse.

Mr Tom Glanville-Jones, defending, had appealed to the Recorder to make a probation order so that Kathryn could continue her studies if allowed to do so by a disciplinary committee of the Law Society. 'This is a young woman who enjoyed a relationship with a much older man of some distinction. It was a relationship with no future. Mr Partridge must have known that, but he was prepared to be selfish about it.'

In January 1992, Kathryn was released from prison and resumed her career as a solicitor after telling reporters: 'I give a new meaning to the term criminal lawyer.'

Since her release she has moved back with her parents in Llangoedmor in a house just a stone's throw from Graham Partridge's farmhouse. The former lovers do not even acknowledge each other in the street.

Kathryn said: 'I want nothing more to do with him. When there is a fundamental breach of trust in a relationship all respect is lost. I don't regret what I did.'

After her spell in prison, Kathryn said she wanted to work in the area of civil-liberties law and to champion prison reform.

'I've changed as a person. I've moved left of the spectrum.'

Devil in Disguise

Even in her jogging pants Lawrencia Bembenek looked stunning. Everything about her was just right. Her face was beautifully structured. Her flowing chestnut-brown hair styled perfectly. Her breasts firm and ample but not too large. Her bottom curved, yet delicate. The perfect all-American 22-year old dream.

But it was her eyes, her eyes that really clinched

it. Huge dark brown seas of sensuality. Always wide open. Always happy. Always looking straight at you. Like the eyes of tentative deer. They had it all and they landed Lawrencia with a nickname that was going to stick for the rest of her life — Bambi. Somehow it summed her up. She had an endearing air of innocence about her, a vulnerability that was incredibly attractive. But there was also an animal cunning — a natural instinct to survive.

She certainly had an extraordinary effect on policeman Fred Schultz. He had met Bambi just a few days earlier at a bar in their home town of Milwaukee. They had struck up a brief and pleasant enough conversation — but no more. Bambi was no easy pick-up for recently divorced older men like Schultz. She did not mind talking to him but that was as far as it would go.

'How about coming jogging with me tomorrow?'

Bambi was taken aback. She had been expecting all the usual lines about coming back to my place but this guy was asking her for a jog. That shy, somewhat icy veneer had been knocked off balance. This was not what she expected. Maybe this guy was genuine?

'Sure. Why not? What time do you want to meet?' Bambi could not believe herself. What was she doing agreeing to go for a jog with a man she did not even know? But there was something about him. He seemed honest. He seemed to really care. In any case, he could hardly attack her while they were jogging.

So they agreed to a date — if that is the way to describe running on the streets of Milwaukee. It was hardly a romantic setting for two would-be lovers, but it seemed appropriate at the time.

The actual jogging part of that first meeting was not exactly informative. As they huffed and puffed their way around a vast park on the edge of the city, there was little energy left for actual conversation. That would come later. For now they were testing each other's physical limitations without even touching. And Bambi was proving the fitter of the two.

She soon found herself racing yards ahead of the 32-year old detective. But he did not care one tiny bit. Being beaten by a woman did not bother Fred Schultz. He was enjoying a completely different aspect of their race through the park. He loved watching her slim and shapely body movements ahead of him. Her buttocks seemed so firm through the skin tight material of her figure-hugging sweat pants.

Fred reckoned he could pant behind that body for the rest of his life. And maybe beyond.

When they finally came to a halt, he could not

take his eyes off her hot, glistening face. Watching the beads of sweat gently roll down her forehead, past those gorgeous eyes onto the perfectly formed cheeks then cascading onto those moist lips before her tongue darted out and licked them away.

Fred Schultz was smitten. He did not even know her full name yet. But this had to be the woman for him. She just had to be.

Then it happened. That spark of coincidence that marks the start of any successful relationship. As Bambi and Fred sat down in a cafe to chat she asked him that classic question.

'What do you do Fred?'

'Oh. I'm a cop. What's your line?'

Bambi stopped in her tracks. For a moment Fred thought it was that old familiar sign of a woman who doesn't like cops. Maybe her father's in jail? Perhaps she's had a run in with the police? It happened so often he just took it for granted. He had hoped and prayed this woman might be different but now it seemed that he was facing the usual anti-police sentiments.

But just the opposite was true.

She sipped her coffee; licked the froth away with her tongue and smiled. 'I used to be a cop too.'

And with those words, Bambi instantly sealed the fate of a relationship that would lead to marriage and so much more besides.

The wedding was a simple affair. They had little money but it cost nothing to choose the most romantic date of the year for the ceremony Valentine's Day, 1981.

Fred had been married before. With an ex-wife Christine and two sons to support, he did not have a lot of spare change at the end of each month. The $363.50 mortgage plus $330 in child support soaked up almost half his detective's take-home salary. It was tough. And Bambi wasn't in the big earnings league either. Working as an aerobics instructor by day and a Playboy Bunny by night, she was struggling to pay off mounting debts.

But they had each other — and that was what mattered most.

Bambi regularly blew her lid about the money Fred was shelling out to Christine and the kids. Here she was marrying an older, successful man but they could hardly afford the rent on a modest one-bedroomed apartment while Christine lived a few blocks away in a lovely detached house. It just did not seem right. But Fred had obligations to keep — and he was a man of his word.

Still, it continued to really grate at Bambi. She could not get it out of her head. Even as they hosted a special gathering of close friends at a dinner party on the evening of the wedding, her mind kept wandering back to it.

'You know. It would pay to have Christine blown away.'

Judy Zess stopped chewing the piece of a chicken in her mouth for a moment. She could not believe what she just heard her old friend and former room-mate Bambi say.

This was the eve of her wedding and she was threatening to 'blow away' her new husband's first wife. What on earth did she mean? It was hardly a healthy start to the marriage. Judy Zess never forgot those few, sinister words. They would one day have a prophetic significance.

Fred Schultz, however, was deliriously happy. He had found himself a beautiful bride to restart his life with. After years of marital grief with Christine, he truly believed he had found the girl of his dreams. Someone he could spend forever with.

He was so besotted, he ignored the sneers of some of his colleagues at work. They remembered Bambi as someone quite different from the pretty, sensual creature he had fallen in love with. They recalled her as being the 'dope head' girl cop who did not charge a pal when she was caught smoking cannabis. In their eyes, she was trouble — and she had shamed her unit by sympathising with druggies.

In fact, they suspected she even smoked marijuana herself. That was one of the reasons they fired her back in 1980.

Bambi had a lot of enemies inside the Milwaukee Police Department:

'She was too darned pretty to be a cop in the first place.'

'Her type should never have joined the force.'

Bambi certainly provoked opinions. She was a person of extremes after all. You either loved her or hated her and Schultz loved her to death. But his fellow colleagues hated her with a vengeance.

Nevertheless, there was one aspect of Bambi that her husband deeply detested — her job at the local Playboy Club. Fred did not care that on a good couple of nights, Bambi could earn the entire month's rent on their modest apartment. He may have been permanently broke but no wife of his was going to work in that place.

Bambi sort of understood her new husband's feelings but she also knew they were financially hard-pressed. In any case, she had a great body. Why not show if off a little and get paid for the pleasure?

'Those guys pay me a $50 tip just so they can look at my body.' Bambi was very matter of fact about it. She would never, ever even consider selling her body for sex. But dressing up in a slinky leotard with a fake bunny tail stuck on her bottom did not seem so bad. In any case, she was proud of her fit, lean body. She knew she had good breasts and gorgeous hips. She did not mind wiggling the right parts if necessary. It was all harmless stuff.

But Fred was adamant. He did not like the idea of all those guys lusting after her — and it was hardly the right sort of career for a policeman's wife. So, after much cajoling, Bambi handed in her bunny's tail and waved goodbye to those, sleazy, risky nights at the Playboy Club. The trouble was that it gave her more time to herself. More time to think. More time to brood. More time to get angry. More time to get vicious.

Fred was working longer and longer hours in his job as a busy crime detective on the streets of Milwaukee. Crime was rife in most neighbourhoods in that gritty, busy city. And that meant Fred and his colleagues really had their work cut out for them.

It also meant a lot of lonely nights at home in front of the television set for Bambi. She could not concentrate on most programmes. Her thoughts were filled with vengeance. Here she was in this tiny, cramped apartment while that woman had a beautiful house. Why? Why was Bambi suffering when she was the one who had just got married?

The only TV shows that diverted her attention were the bleak crime movies. The grisly murders that keep viewers gripped to their seats in terror. They did not scare Bambi. They just made her start to wonder .

The evening of May 27, 1981, was hot and steamy in Milwaukee. But that did not affect Christine Schultz and her two sons Sean, 11, and Shannon, 7. The children were comfortably tucked up in the air-conditioned bedroom of the family's well-maintained detached home in one of the city's better Southside suburbs.

As 30-year old Christine kissed them gently goodnight and left the bedroom, her thoughts could not have been further from the happiness of her ex-husband and his new, young wife. She could only recall the unhappy years with Fred. The arguing. The fighting. The tears. Now, at last she could get on with her new life. A new lover and even the chance of a fresh, happier marriage eventually.

She watched her boys as they drifted into sleep. Life would come good for them, she was sure of it. A thunderous roar broke overhead as a huge airliner made its descent to the nearby airport at Mitchell Field, but they slept through it, safe in a cocoon of dreams.

Christine quietly tip-toed out of their room and headed towards the bedroom she once shared with Fred. A peaceful night in front of the television. She could think of nothing nicer.

Settled into the comfy double divan, she propped herself up with three pillows and immersed herself in one of her favourite shows — M*A*S*H*. Christine laughed out loud at the hilarious adventures of Radar and all the rest of the gang who starred in the top-rating programme. She loved the show's harsh, cynical humour. The reality of it appealed to her. But the real world outside was about to swallow her up forever.

It was 2.20am when little Sean stirred from his deep slumber. At first he thought he was dreaming. He could feel something cold, almost damp, pressing over his face and mouth. Then he felt a choking sensation as if a cord were tightening around his neck.

This was no dream. This was the ultimate nightmare. For a split second, he kept his eyes tightly closed. Hoping that if he did so then it would all go away. But he was having trouble breathing now and his throat felt as if it were about to explode. He had to open his eyes. There was no other possible means of escape.

So he did, and there was terror in its truest form. No goblins, no wicked witches, no make-believe video that sent shivers down your spine but you could laugh at later. Just a leather gloved hand clasping, pressing down on his face. Then another hand, fumbling for a second then pulling a cord tight around his neck. Sean's first scream was muffled. Then his assailant loosened the pressure momentarily so that the noose around his neck could be pulled even tighter.

Just one more breath Sean told himself as his world began to go blurry at the edges through lack of oxygen. He let out an ear-piercing shriek. It was his only chance. His last one. Sean put his entire little body and spirit into that yell and it had the desired effect. The intruder ran out of the room.

What was happening?

The two boys lay there too afraid to move at first. They just did not know what to do. Maybe they should just go back to sleep and then they would wake up in the morning to find it never really happened?

Boom. Boom.

It sounded like a firecracker going off in their mother's bedroom. The boys froze with fear. The reality of that attack moments earlier had now dawned on them utterly and completely. They ran to the bedroom. The bedroom where once they had rushed to sleep with their mother and father whenever they had a bad dream. Now they were about to encounter the worst type of nightmare — reality.

But their protective instincts towards their mother were paramount in their minds at that moment. As they dashed across the hallway they encountered the worst piece of evidence imaginable as a tall, shadowy figure pushed past them towards the stairs and the front door.

They found her face down on the bed. A sight no person should ever have to witness, let alone two small children. There in that bedroom they faced the aftermath of murder — and the victim was their mother.

A clothes line was tied around one hand. She had obviously put up a struggle. In her right shoulder was a gaping gunshot wound, flesh ripped away to the bone. But it was the blue bandanna gagging her mouth that was the most startling sight. It seemed to contort her face into a thousand lines of fear. Thankfully, her eyes were closed so neither of those innocent children had to see the horror etched permanently within.

But how can a child react to such a horrendous scene? They are not emotionally mature enough to know how to cope. Why should they be prepared by their parents for such a terrifying situation? No-one expects it to happen to them.

Sean aged ten years in those first few seconds as he stood in front of his mother's bloodied body. He tried desperately to stop the blood spreading from

Christine's shoulder wound. Thank goodness he did not try to move her body because then he would have seen the full extent of that wound — caused by a single .38 bullet shot at point blank range in her back. It had glanced off her shoulder blade and gone through her heart. She never stood a chance. But it was better this way. At least Sean did not have to look at the graphic nature of the bullet's journey through his mother's body.

As Shannon stood by watching in a terrified trance, Sean struggled vainly to stop the blood from draining out of Christine's body. So often she had been the one to dab his cuts and bruises. She had kissed them better when they hurt like hell. She had covered the cuts with plaster to stop them dripping blood. She had loved and cared for him whatever the circumstances.

Now he was bravely trying to return the previous eleven years of love and attention. But no matter how hard he tried, there was nothing he could do to save her. There was no ebbing life to preserve. She had gone before they even reached the room.

A few minutes later, the shaking, quivering youngster called his mother's boyfriend, policeman Stu Honeck, who lived around the corner.

The cops arrived within minutes.

'It's just not fair Mike. I can hardly afford the price

of a pair of shoes.'

Fred Schultz was complaining to his partner, Det Michael Durfee, about that alimony yet again. Day in day out, the same old story. It was getting too much.

They were filing a burglary report when Fred picked up the ringing phone at their desk. Within moments, his face went white. His eyes began to well up with tears and then he dropped the telephone and left it hanging there.

Fred had just been told that his ex-wife — the mother of his two young sons — had been brutally murdered. He was in a daze. He did not know what to do. He just sat there slumped on his desk, his head in his hands sobbing. There was nothing his partner or anyone else could say. But he did have Bambi to turn to. She was still there. She would support him. She would help him cope. He had to turn to somebody.

Peep. Peep. Peep. Peep .

The line at their home was engaged. What was Bambi doing on the telephone at 2.40 in the morning? Fred was puzzled. He needed her support. Her love. And she was on the phone. Why?

Finally he got through.

'Laurie, wake up! Chris has been shot. She's dead. I'll call you back when I can.'

Bambi said later she thought it was all a dream

when Fred called her. But in fact, she was the instigator of the worst nightmare of all.

'He was a big guy with browny red type of hair and a pony tail.'

Sean had somehow regained enough composure to describe to detectives what the intruder looked like — less than an hour after the awful incident occurred.

The youngster told them he was wearing a baggy, green army jacket and black, police-type shoes. And a green jogging suit. And the gun, the gun had a silver pearl handle.

At least the detectives had something to go on.

'I'm sorry Fred but I got to see if your gun has been fired recently.'

Fred Schultz was stunned. His ex-wife had been murdered just a few hours earlier and now his partner Mike Durfee was at his front door suggesting that his own gun might have been used in the killing.

'What the fuck is this?' he screamed.

Mike gulped, he had to do it — but the despair on his friend's face .

All he could manage in response was, 'It's just a formality.'

Bambi watched coolly as her husband and his partner carefully checked the gun. Durfee found dust on the hammer and sniffed for any tell-tale signs of gunpowder odour. There was nothing. This weapon had not been used for quite some time.

'Look Fred. What can I say? It had to be checked.' Fred nodded slowly. Deep down, he understood the reasons behind his partner's visit. In fact, he felt fairly relieved because he knew who they would all be pointing the finger of suspicion at — his beautiful new young wife.

Bambi did not bat an eyelid. She looked as sexy and seductive as ever when they finally climbed into bed together to try and snatch a few hours sleep.

Policemen have a well-known coldness when it comes to death. They encounter it so frequently that they soon become emotionally divorced from the reality of all the normal responses it provokes.

'It's just a body. It's not someone you know and love so it means nothing.'

An everyday occurrence. If it starts getting to you it's time to get out. But sometimes, inevitably, there are occasions when it hits home. The death of Christine Schultz should have been one of those occasions. Yet, bizarrely, Fred had recovered his composure completely by the time he was summoned to the city morgue to formally identify his ex-wife's body.

The cop and his pretty young ex-cop wife walked into the cold, sterile room as if they had been there a thousand times before. And they had. But surely this time it was different? They were about to see the brutally-slain corpse of the woman who bore him two children. It had to be a difficult moment for any person — surely?

'Hey Laurie look at the size of this wound will you?' Bambi was astonished. Whatever her true feelings towards the woman who lay on that morgue slab, she hardly felt in the mood to start passing medical comments on the size of the wounds.

But Fred was insistent.

'Come on Laurie. You saw enough stiffs when you were in the force.' As it happened Bambi had not been 'in the force' for very long and she managed to avoid seeing too many 'stiffs'. But that was irrelevant. She felt reluctant to go near that corpse. She did not want to face the reality of the situation. It frightened her.

Still Fred persisted. For a good few minutes he stood examining the fatal wound that had rubbed out his ex-wife's life.

'Wow! That's some wound.'

Bambi could not take this gruesome verbal post mortem another moment longer. She left Fred alone with his ex-wife for the one and only time.

Cops investigating Christine's tragic slaying were baffled. All their enquiries kept leading them to

Bambi. She had told so many people of her dislike for Christine. The threats were commonplace, the envy an open secret. But so far they had not a shred of evidence.

Even Fred began to wonder. He took a pretty active role in the investigation. Some of his more cynical colleagues suggested it was to hide his own guilt. But it was becoming more and more apparent to Fred that Bambi certainly had the motive, if not the means.

There were no witnesses to place Bambi outside of that apartment on that night in May. But she had access to the off-duty gun Fred kept at home and the keys to the house where his ex-wife lived. There was no sign of forced entry by the murderer. Then the cops got a break of sorts. They found a reddish brown wig in the toilet system at Bambi's apartment block. A brown synthetic hair recovered from Christine Schultz's leg was very similar to the fibres from that wig. Then they discovered a hair recovered from the gag in Christine's mouth was not unlike Bambi's.

But it was still nothing concrete. The cops knew that Fred's gun had to hold the key. But it had already been tested by his partner the night of the murder.

On June 18 — a full three weeks after the murder — Fred, accompanied by Det James Gauger, picked up his off-duty revolver for test firing at the state crime lab.

Once again, Bambi looked on coolly as her husband and his colleague took away what was to become their most damning piece of evidence.

After stringent tests it was found to have been the gun that killed Christine.

On June 24, 1981, Lawrencia Bembenek was arrested and charged with the murder of Christine Schultz.

At a Milwaukee court in February, 1982, Bambi was sentenced to life for the killing. It took the jury three and a half days of deliberation and circuit judge Michael Skwierawski called it 'the most circumstantial case I have ever seen.'

A campaign was mounted to get the decision overturned but all subsequent appeals failed.

Then, in August 1990, Bambi escaped from the Tay-cheedah Women's Correctional Institute in Wisconsin. She was helped by the handsome brother of another woman inmate. And the two proclaimed their love for one another before she made her daring escape.

Incredibly, the attractive ex-policewoman was still protesting her innocence when she was arrested in Thunder Bay, Ontario, Canada, three months later. She had got a job as a waitress and was living under a false name with her lover.

Just before her escape, Bambi was asked by a journalist what she would do in her first hour of freedom. She replied: 'Have sex.'

Blind Fury

Christine English hated the mornings.

There was always so much to do. Get the kids ready for school. Make sure they ate some breakfast. Do the beds. Tidy the house. A never-ending stream of chores.

And then there was Barry.

Once both her sons had departed for school, she had to nursemaid him through the morning. In some ways, he was more like another child than her lover.

They had been together for four years. But sometimes it felt like four hundred. Their love for each other veered from hatred to total infatuation — and there was no knowing which way it would end.

All her friends kept telling her she was mad to set up home with a man six years her junior, but Barry kept Christine feeling young. When he wanted to be, he could be the most loving, caring person in the world.

She didn't want to listen to what everyone was saying. So long as the good times were more frequent than the bad, she was happy.

Lately, however, she had begun to wonder whether it really was all worth it. Barry had turned to drink in a big way. It started with beers every night in the pub but, in the past year or so, he had found a taste for vodka.

Nearly every night he would end up drunk or close to it. Sometimes he was amusing company when he was tipsy, other times he turned into an out-of-control monster who would strike real fear into Christine.

Barry's problems lay with his work. Like so many self-employed people he was under enormous financial strain. He owned a franchise to a bakery. Although the business was doing OK, it wasn't bringing in the return Barry had once hoped for.

Life had turned into a constant battle for him. His only way out was the bottle. When he was drinking none of the stresses and strains, however large, would enter his mind.

In the pub of an evening, he would sit at the bar, talking to his drinking partners about everything except his business. It was a great way to avoid the tensions. Drink was the great escape.

When Barry got home to Christine each night, he would start to sober up and realise that what he was doing was merely a smokescreen for his problems. Underneath it all, he was well aware that he couldn't just carry on pickling his brain in alcohol.

He had to do something to sort himself out. But how? Christine knew the answer, but she didn't know how she was going to convince Barry. Many years before, after the birth of her two sons, she had noticed her moods swinging enormously in the space of just a few hours. At first she just dismissed it as temporary post-natal depression. The man she was married to then had not helped. He wasn't interested in her 'women's problems'.

'What are you on about woman,' he'd grumble, an uncomprehending scowl on his face. Their marriage was already crumbling, so compassion did not come high on his list of emotional priorities.

Christine was desperate to break out of the constant moods that were starting to make her life miserable. Sometimes she would get so het up she would start smashing up cutlery, throwing it around the kitchen in an inexplicable frenzy.

Afterwards, she would try to explain to her husband why it had happened. But he didn't want to know.

'He just did not care. A woman's place was clearly defined in his little world and the sort of problems I had were the sort he did not want to talk about,' explained Christine later.

Things got worse and worse at home for Christine. The moods became more frequent and less controllable. It was as if there was a different person inside her, trying desperately to get out and cause havoc.

After one particularly nasty fight with her husband, she threw a plate at him. He struck her. That was it. She had to do something before it was too late.

So Christine turned to Transcendental Meditation. It was the mid-seventies. Hippies had come and almost gone — yesterday's beatniks were today's married couples with 2.2 kids — but TM was a relic that had survived the fickle swings of fashion. It was also the life saver Christine had been looking for. At first, she attended group meetings where everyone would sit and meditate. Learn to relax in a way the modern world rarely allows you to.

Christine was given her own mantra. It was a call-sign awarded to her by her teacher. A name that no-one else in the entire world should ever know — or be called. Her teacher warned her of the dire consequences if she ever revealed her mantra to anyone else.

Within weeks, she began to feel better. Just meditating for fifteen minutes every morning before breakfast and just before bed seemed to calm her so much. She was starting to look inside herself more, to understand the powers that were making her so tense, appreciating the evil influences that were contributing to her unhappiness. Christine was starting to find an answer.

It had given her hope for the future and made her far more tolerant and understanding towards Barry's drink problems than she ever would have been with her husband.

When Barry's boozing became excessive she knew she would have to use her TM experiences to help him escape from his problems — just as she herself had done all those years before.

'In any case, Barry wanted it. He was desperate to sort himself out,' explained Christine.

One night he wept in her arms, after a particularly outrageous drinking bout, and begged her to help him find the same sort of contentment as her.

He refused to attend a TM session. He wanted Christine to teach him. No-one else was trustworthy enough. He was like a child in that way, feeling he could not do it in front of strangers. Immature reservations aside, he was desperate to rid himself of his problems before they cost him his life.

Naturally, Christine was troubled by all this. She felt that he should attend proper classes but she knew something had to be done quickly, otherwise it might be too late. What she feared most of all was that superstition about the mantra. He wanted her mantra. Nobody else's. In fact he insisted that Christine shared that name with him as a pre-condition to learning TM.

Barry needed to be helped so badly. He wanted to sort himself out and Christine loved him.

Reluctantly, she agreed to tell him. It was something that would haunt her forever.

Only the night before, they had had such a great evening together. It had been like old times really. Lots of cuddles. Lots of love. Lots of security.

Christine had felt, for the first time in many months, that maybe they could survive together. Barry was meditating regularly with her now. It actually seemed to be working.

Maybe all that superstition about the mantra was nonsense. Perhaps he really would start to live a decent life again. Barry had started to take the TM as seriously as Christine. Every morning they would meditate together. It was having a calming influence. She hoped it would start to divert him away from the drink.

She had gone to sleep that night feeling really optimistic. It certainly made a change.

But the next morning, Christine felt she was back at square one. All that happiness and contentment had disappeared to be replaced with a searing feeling of tension coming from deep inside herself.

However, Barry was not the instigator this time.

The cause of her depression was far more simple, although just as tragic. Christine was about to start her menstrual cycle — and she felt awful.

Over the years, Christine had got used to suffering really badly. The TM had helped enormously but PMT was still something she dreaded. While many women manage to carry on their lives virtually unaffected, Christine really couldn't cope.

That pre-menstrual stage would build up until she felt like snapping with the tension. In the week or so before her period she would suffer from splitting head-aches, swelling parts of the body, pimples on her skin and incredibly tender breasts. Headaches are often referred to as the body's all-purpose distress signal. They alert you to the fact that something is wrong. In Christine's case, they were throbbing and excrutiatingly painful, like a hot knife going right through the temple.

Swollen breasts are often a woman's only symptom of Pre-Menstrual Tension. But, in Christine's case, they were just part of the agonising scenario. Any hug or pressure was painful. It made her sound irritated, even when she was not. And it didn't help in any relationship with an ignorant man. Then there was the weight gain and bloating that often accompanied the PMT. Sometimes she would put on as much as seven pounds — all as a result of her body's retention of water.

Her skin also became pink and blotchy. Boils and cold sores were frequent occurrences for Christine. These would affect her confidence and, in turn, could make her even snappier.

Worst of all, though, was the clumsiness. Things were always falling out of Christine's hands. She was forever walking into furniture and knocking things over. Most of the time she would blame herself for her awkwardness. That would put her under even, more pressure. Her previous husband and now Barry never truly understood why.

There lay Christine's biggest problem.

The men in her life just never seemed to appreciate the pain and anguish she went through. They just dismissed her behaviour as 'bloody irritating'. Never bothering to really try to think about what was happening inside her body.

She suffered constant anxiety or panic attacks. She felt unloved, irritable, always on the defensive. She would lash out at people for no reason and find herself bursting into tears at the slightest provocation. Even when Barry bought her a present, she would scream at him for no apparent reason.

Then there was the depression. Moodiness, no interest in people or important events, lack of energy, lack of concentration, forgetfulness, insomnia. It all seemed to gang up on Christine and no amount of TM could completely cure her of it. But at least it relaxed her enough to make her believe she could cope.

When she meditated, her body seemed to float away from all the tensions surrounding her. For a precious quarter-hour, she could lose herself in a sea of mysticism. It was the ultimate escape. Sometimes, she wished she could do it permanently.

But the moment she woke up on December 16, 1980, she knew it was going to be a very difficult day — thanks to PMT.

That tense feeling was in her head as she grappled for

the alarm clock. It could only get worse.

At least she would have Barry for support. Surely he would be understanding about her problem this time? He had witnessed her foul tempers enough in the past. When she tried to explain to him what was going on, he started to appreciate the anguish she went through every month. But it was clear that he did not really understand.

On this particular morning, Barry wasn't in such a good mood himself. Although he had happily soothed Christine the whole of the night before, resulting in a pleasant evening together, he had something he wanted to tell her. And he didn't think she'd like it. She'd only been up a few minutes and she was already very stressed out.

As she meditated in the corner of the bedroom that morning, the TM helped ease the anxiety, but she still had the whole day ahead to cope with.

They meditated together, hoping a 15 minute trance at the end of the bed might be the answer to both their problems. But Barry had not been concentrating properly. Christine noticed he had other things on his mind.

The anticipation of the argument he was bound to provoke was already making Barry short-tempered — and he hadn't even told her yet.

He'd let her get the kids off to school before he

broke it to her. Otherwise, she would really go to pieces — and that would not be fair on the children. Barry had a sense of right and wrong. Maybe that was why he was so worried about telling Christine his little secret. In the time they had been together, she had proved to be remarkably possessive. She didn't like any other female even so much as looking at Barry.

He was her's — and no-one else's. That was her attitude and she was sticking to it.

Even when he began drinking more and more and staying at the pub until almost midnight, Christine still regarded him as her property; she was always wary of the predators circling around him. She knew she had to keep a pretty close eye on him. But Barry was not so keen. He liked the idea of being attractive to other women; it was good for his ego. Besides, it didn't have to mean he slept with them. Being admired is a far cry from infidelity.

He didn't like her possessiveness. It intruded on his freedom, stopped him being a lad about town.

'I'm going to meet another woman tonight.'

Barry spluttered out the words as hurriedly as possible. It was as if he knew he had to tell her but was hoping she wouldn't hear him.

Christine heard him all right. She looked up from the breakfast table at her handsome lover. She was momentarily stunned. What the hell was he saying? They had just enjoyed one of their best evenings together in months and he was now telling her he was going out with another woman.

She was numbed. He wouldn't do that. He couldn't! Why did he want to hurt her? What right had he to treat her like this?

The tension increased by the second as his words began to sink in. Christine could feel the tightness in her stomach as the adrenaline pumped around her veins, making even her finger tips stiffen with anger.

She began to shout at Barry. How could he do such a thing? Didn't he love her? Bastard. Bastard. Bastard.

She would not let him. It was as simple as that. She would not allow him to see the other woman. He would have to make his choice: If he chose this woman then he may as well not bother coming back that night, or any other for that matter.

But Barry was adamant. He wanted his freedom. She could not stand in his way.

He stormed out of the house.

'I am going to run him over. I am going to run him over.'

Christine English kept repeating it to herself over and over again. The elderly woman at the other end of the line was understandably perturbed — she was Barry Kitson's mother.

'I am going to kill him. I am going to run him over and kill him.'

Christine was adamant. The strain that had been building up inside her all day was fast reaching breaking point.

She had eaten nothing but half a sandwich at lunch-time. For a woman who suffered from severe PMT this was madness. All medical researches on PMT have long agreed on one thing — skipping meals can often worsen the symptoms. The irony is that cutting back on food is a classic response to tension and unhappiness. But the lack of food, when nourishment is sorely needed, can be particularly hazardous.

It was mid-afternoon and Christine was already at the end of her tether. She had to tell someone what she felt — so why not his mother?

Mrs Kitson knew that things between them were not good and that her son was partly to blame, but she listened in horror to Christine's threats.

Christine couldn't concentrate on anything. Her mind kept going back to Barry. She wasn't going to let him betray her with that woman. Not tonight. Not any night.

At home that afternoon she was close to tears

as she prepared tea for her two sons on their return from school.

How could he just announce his decision like that? How could he be so uncaring? After all she'd done for him.

Christine sat with her head in her hands wondering what she should do about it. In the back of her mind she kept recalling the words she shrieked hysterically at his mother: 'I am going to run him over. I am going to run him over.'

Maybe that was the answer.

By the time Barry got home in the evening, Christine felt her life had been systematically broken into little pieces. Everything she relied on to help her through times of crisis had vanished without explanation. The foundations had been dismantled from beneath her feet.

When he walked in, she tried to stay calm but it was no good. She could not bottle up the anger and bitterness she felt toward him. And to make matters worse, he was still determined to go ahead with his date with another woman. They were heading for an inevitable collision.

'How can you do it? How can you?' She broke the silence within minutes of him settling down in an armchair in the living room.

'I've had enough of this. I'm off.'

Barry made for the door. Desperate to find an escape route away from the constant pressure being applied by Christine. He took the only course of action he knew — and went straight to the pub.

The Live And Let Live was the perfect retreat for Barry Kitson, and it had a particularly pertinent name for him that night. It was the sort of place where he could lose himself in a sea of alcohol. Somewhere to forget his troubles. A pub where he could be himself.

With it's beige, nicotine-stained walls and swirling red carpet, the Trueman's Ales pub was typical of the sort of bar found in a provincial English town. A dart board offered the only exercise of the day to any regulars.

Barry took up his stool against the tatty pine-clad bar it gave a clear view through the window to the car park outside.

When Christine turned up that evening, she didn't even have to go into the pub for Barry to know she had arrived.

She walked in and tried to nag at him in front of his drinking mates. He was embarrassed and intensely irritated.

'Leave me alone woman.'

He did not want to know. In any case, he still had that date with the other woman to go to.

Christine knew that only too well, but she was

determined to try to do something to stop it. But the more he drank, the more obsessed Barry became with his inflated idea of freedom. Really, he wanted to see lots of other women the whole time. This was just an excuse to start playing around. Deep down, they both knew that.

Christine really did care about his welfare. She wanted him to come home and sleep off the drink. She hoped he'd forget about the other woman and they could start afresh in the morning.

'Well. If you won't come home, I'll drive you there,' Christine finally offered.

It was a bizarre way to respond, but she was convinced that so long as she was near him there was a chance he might give up his plans for the night.

The journey was strained. After all, Christine was driving her lover to meet another woman on a date. Her motivation was bewildering. Most wives or lovers would have kicked their partner out long ago. But Christine lived in hope that they would enjoy a normal, peaceful life together.

The anxiety was building up inside all the time. She was shaking with tension. She was making herself suffer.

When they arrived, Barry got out of the car without uttering a word and walked towards the pub where his secret lover was supposed to be waiting.

As Christine sat in the car outside the pub, it

really began to dawn on her what a fool she was being.

Why had she allowed herself to drive him to meet another woman? How could he humiliate her so much?

She sat in the car outside the pub with her eyes closed. Trying to clear her mind. Trying to get a hold of herself. See sense. This was all so ridiculous.

She loved him so much, but what on earth was she doing waiting for him? He was probably inside there holding the bitch's hand while she sat in that car just a few yards away.

People kept walking past her car, wondering what she was doing. She ignored their stares, determined to wait for him however long it took.

After nearly thirty minutes Barry emerged. He was alone. She felt a surge of relief go through her body. He had been stood up for his date. Christine was ecstatic. Barry was furious.

She saw it as a victory. He looked enraged. It was a humiliating climb-down. He was the one who looked a fool now. He had been let down by one woman. Now he had to face the full wrath of another.

Even the drink was beginning to wear off. Even the headaches had been transferred to him.

In the car there was a tense silence. Christine was still outraged by his insulting behaviour. But at least she had her man back. Barry was sulking. It was inevitable they would end up rowing. He called her a bitch. He reckoned she was sneering because she was so satisfied at his failure to pull.

In truth, Christine was far from satisfied. She was angered by his remarks. He was trying to turn the tables on her. Make her feel guilty about the fact that he had a secret rendezvous with another woman Her head was throbbing with pain again. It felt as though a tight band of steel was squeezing her skull. Bright light slammed into her eyes, loud noises hammered at her ear-drums, the lightest of touches felt they would bruise. To top it all, she felt nauseously dizzy.

It was Barry, however, who cracked first. He grabbed her hair, slapping her viciously across the face. She pulled the car up and started to fight back. Desperate to hurt him. To make him pay for all the awful things he had done to her.

She blasted the horn.

'Get out... get out...'

Barry carried on hitting her. But then he noticed they had just pulled up near another of his favourite pubs. He got out of the car. Slammed the door and marched off towards the entrance.

He warned her not to follow him. He said he just wanted to be left alone or 'I'll call the cops.'

Barry must have sensed the devil lurking inside

Christine's mind as he walked away.

Christine was shaking with fear at her own rage. She felt incensed by his behaviour. Hurt. Fury. Hate. She had all those feelings going through her head. She had to stop him treating her like this. It could not go on. She kept remembering the warnings of her friends and family. 'He's a bad type. What are you doing with him?' they used to say.

She felt an urge to drive after him. To punish him for all those hurtful things he had done. Flatten him into a bloody pulp forever.

She started up the car and drove after him. She wanted to damage him.

As the car approached him, he turned and faced her. Defiant. Full of bravado.

She looked into his eyes and realised she could not harm the man she loved, so she pulled away and just drove around and around Colchester instead. She needed time to think. She had to get a grip on herself. But the heartbreak of the situation just would not release it's grip on her. One moment she felt compassion and love for him, the next she would feel a burning desire to make him suffer, just as he had made her suffer.

Christine thought that, by driving around, she might be able to work off the aggression. She had been so close to killing him. She had to get that feeling out of her system.

But Colchester has only a small core. Soon, she found herself driving past pub after pub that she knew Barry would go to.

It was inevitable that she would come across him wandering drunkenly out of one. She drove through the town's one-way system. Then she signalled right, back onto the dual carriage way that skirts the edge of the town centre.

It was a repetitious journey. The constant driving was soon interrupted when she spotted Barry. Christine immediately felt that uncontrollable surge of tension returning, when she laid eyes on him.

She stopped the car by him and they began arguing. This time, it was a ferocious row with no limit to the insults they were hurling at each other. All the time, Christine could feel the knots in her stomach tightening.

The enormous stress was exacerbating the symptoms of PMT. She desperately needed to find a way to ease her pain. All that meditation had helped. But, as she sat there; she realised it had not really gone to the root of her problems. The break-down of every meaningful relationship she'd ever had.

Why did she feel so bad? Why did all this have to happen now, just at the most crucial time? Why couldn't she just close her eyes and wake up somewhere pleasant instead of sitting in that car fighting?

'Just go away!' Barry was yelling at the top of his voice now.

Christine felt a strange compulsion to chase after him. She wanted to wind the argument up even more. She wanted it to reach a crescendo from which there could be no return.

Barry was already at breaking point. He seemed about to explode as he sat in the car next to her.

Without any warning he hit her on the head with his hand. It was a short, sharp movement. He did it again. This time smashing down on her arm instead.

She tried desperately to fight back, but he was far too strong for her. They were virtually wrestling inside the car now.

Then Barry drew out his ultimate weapon. Something that would hurt her more than any punch. The threat to end all threats. Something he knew she dreaded.

'I never want to see you again.'

He slammed the car door shut and walked off.

She watched him for a moment. In her terrible state, everything seemed distorted with the streetlights and shadows and colours from the buildings and roads all converging on her, rushing towards her as though they would smack the windscreen.

Then she realised the car was moving. She felt herself press down on the accelerator.

I am going to run him over... I am going to run him over. Then a little voice inside her head said. I'm hungry! But it was too late for that now. The only thing she could feed on was revenge.

It was meant to be. Never tell anyone the name of your mantra. It will only bring misery to your life.

He knew her inner-most secrets. Now fate would take a hand and punish him for that knowledge.

Run him down! Run him down! Flatten the bastard! The evil little voice had to have it's say.

Christine watched Barry as he half walked, half stumbled along the street.

Do it. Go on. He deserves it!

Barry was about to cross the entrance to Sainsbury's. He never got there.

She felt the urge to press harder on the accelerator pedal. She tried to pull her foot up, but the twitching became even worse. She wanted to slam her foot hard down.

It's so easy. Bye bye unhappiness — just one small step...

Barry helped make up her mind. He turned and, looking straight at her, thrust two fingers into the air. Fuck you, they said, you wouldn't dare.

Christine took a deep breath and pressed her foot down as hard as possible on the accelerator. Just a little bump to show him. That'll shut him up.

Barry didn't believe she would actually do it. She didn't have it in her.

As he stumbled across the poorly-lit entrance to Sainsbury's, he turned and saw her face. She certainly looked determined. But she wouldn't actually kill him. He'd test her bottle. And laugh at her when she slammed on the brakes.

The front of the car hit Barry with a huge thud. Then he was swept on to the bonnet.

The bulk of his body lolled against the windscreen.

She felt no emotion. Just a determination to finish off the job properly. She could have stopped there and then. He was already badly injured. Instead, she kept her foot full down on the accelerator and mounted the pavement before smashing head-on into a telegraph pole.

The impact of the car jolted Christine out of her intense trance. She heard her lover groaning. The man she had slept with just ten hours earlier. The man she had just tried to kill.

He was pinned between the lamp-post and the car bonnet, his right leg was almost severed.

'Get it off me. Get it off me.' His voice was

slight and agonising.

'Get it off me. Get...'

He was fading by the second.

Christine English sat for a moment behind the wheel of the car, unable, for a second, to absorb the enormity of what she had just done. Then hysteria took over. It was all so unreal.

'Please, please tell me it's not true. Please God, it hasn't happened.'

Christine stood by the side of the car now. She kept telling herself she only meant to frighten him. She did not want to do this.

Two weeks later Barry Kitson died in hospital.

Christine English was given a conditional discharge for twelve months after pleading guilty to manslaughter with diminished responsibility when she appeared before Norwich Crown Court.

Before deciding to free her, Judge Justice Perchas said, 'There is no course of treatment which can be prescribed for you. But now you are aware that a dramatically minor affair like eating properly is of the utmost importance.'

Retribution

The house was simple. Plain bricks. Sloping roof. Nothing too elaborate. It was a bungalow with an abundance of windows but not much character. Set back off the road, its stark, square, modern look made it more in keeping with the suburbs of Los Angeles, than an isolated part of mid-Wales.

It rained a lot in the tiny hamlet of Pant Perthog. The grey clouds and harsh gusts of wind were a permanent feature of life for the handful of residents, yet the climate only helped to emphasize the beauty of the terrain. Lush, rolling hills strewn with acres of ancient woodlands surrounded the village. It was a picture postcard spot where little had changed for over a century.

Just fifty yards to the rear of the bungalow lay the real reason it had been built in the first place. The River Dovey twisted and turned as it snaked a path through the Welsh countryside. Splitting fields in two. Creating bushy river banks amongst little clumps of trees. Providing an excuse for a scattering of those curved, grey stone bridges built so lovingly by the Victorians.

Most properties in the area had their own names like Pear Tree Cottage or Alamo. But the bungalow that Wanda Chantler lived in had no name. Its very existence was enough for her. It was her home.

She would have been happy to hide herself away in that house from the world outside. She had no interest in other people. Just eternal gratitude for being alive and well after a life steeped in tragedy.

Wanda and her husband Alan had deliberately chosen the isolated area of Machynlleth as their home because they wanted the peace and solitude that had always eluded them. They really needed the quietness. Both of them had, for too long, been influenced by events that were out of their control. They did not want that any more. They wanted to be in charge of their own destiny.

Wanda had lovingly planned every detail of the construction of the house with her husband Alan 20 years earlier. It became their sanctuary. Their own little piece of paradise in an evil world. An escape from the unspeakable atrocities that occured every day somewhere on the globe. A place where they could bring up their two sons without worry.

And that is what they did. As a family, they became a self-contained unit. Just the four of them. They didn't bother the world and it didn't bother them. They loved to explore the countryside on long rambling walks. Sometimes they would travel to the coast and enjoy a picnic on deserted beaches facing the Atlantic.

But then they made a mistake. A big mistake. After the kids had grown up, they made the heart-wrenching decision to sell the bungalow and head off to Australia to be with one of their sons. It had seemed like the perfect opportunity to come out of their shell-like existance in Pant Perthog and to start to rediscover the outside world. Their plans had failed miserably. Outside of that tiny retreat, they found that nothing had changed.

The same evil forces dominated. The same

problems existed. The same wars ravaged on. It was all a bitter disappointment to the Chantlers. They had really hoped and prayed that the new, modern world might be more welcoming. But it was not to be.

Australia wasn't right for them. The idea of sun, sand and sea just did not appeal. The gentle waves of the mid-Wales coastline were a far nicer proposition than the giant surf of Bondi Beach. They felt out of place in an alien world where nearly everyone was under forty.

Wanda, fifty-seven years old, was a highly articulate woman. She always appeared a little dishevelled in a friendly sort of way. She had an intense, introvert manner much of the time. Always slightly on her guard but basically full of good intentions. A trained physiotherapist and a linguist with nine languages to her credit, she found Australia a shallow place. She had little in common with the people she met. She longed to look once more at those lush pastures of Pant Perthog.

Her favourite hobby was painting. She just wanted to have an opportunity to use her water colours to once more re-create that stunning scenery. Back at the bungalow, she used to spend hours lovingly producing her own interpretations of the surrounding countryside. She could lose herself in the paintings. Forget about those painful memories.

Only think about the beautiful things in life and put them on canvas.

Alan, just turned 60, felt just as uncomfortable as his wife in the so-called 'New World' of Australia. Bespectacled and still with a reasonable head of hair, he was an average looking character. He knew full well how happy Wanda would be to come back to mid-Wales. It meant so much to them both. They were convinced they would feel an immense warmness the moment they arrived once more in the area. They kept wondering why on earth they had sold up their dream to take on a nightmare? It was for the love of the children of course. But they had both grown up by now. They had their own lives to lead. Wanda and Alan needed to get on without them. It would all be so much easier back where they belonged.

So, it was no surprise when Wanda and Alan decided to leave Australia and return to mid-Wales in the late 1970s.

They were so relieved when they arrived back in the area. So delighted to see all those old familiar sights. So enchanted by the slow pace of life. So pleased by the easy-going nature of the people. Nothing appeared to have changed.

Everyone welcomed them back to Pant Perthog as if they had never been away in the first place. That pleasant feeling of warm security began to return as they settled back in the area.

It was so much nicer than Australia. There was a post office and a little shop in the village. Nothing more, nothing less. It was definitely meant to be.

They loved to be able to wander up and down the lanes without that fear of the unknown. The fear they had been haunted by more than 30 years earlier. The fear that returned when they went to live in Australia.

As far as Wanda was concerned, only one thing was still missing. She longed to have that bungalow back. She was desperate to live once again in the place she had been so happy. On the journey back to mid-Wales she kept telling Alan how wonderful it would be to buy the house once again. It held so many cherished memories. He was just as keen, but he feared it might not be as easy as all that.

Wanda's dream really kept her going. She imagined herself back there with all the happy memories of the children.

New owners Roger and Josie Hartland were delighted when they bought the bungalow from the Chantlers. They saw it as their home for the rest of their lives. In much the same way as the Chantlers once had, they envisaged staying there for ever.

There was something about the area. It was so pure and simple. There were so few complications...

until Wanda Chantler returned.

It had been a dream come true for the Hartlands when they bought the place. Roger, 48, had decided he wanted to quit the rat-race and leave his job as an industrial chemist in the Midlands. He couldn't stand the relentless high-pressure existence. Pant Perthog seemed the perfect location and his young wife was just as convinced they were doing the right thing.

They loved the Chantlers' taste. They admired the way they had managed to make a very plain-looking house incredibly warm and cosy inside. It had a vital, airy atmosphere. Something that instantly attracted Roger and Josie when they were looking for a home to retire to.

They even felt grateful to the Chantlers for creating such a perfect home and fully appreciated just how heart breaking it had been for them to move out. They tried to reassure them on their move to Australia to join their son.

'It's supposed to be a lovely place. You'll soon settle there.'

But the Chantlers' obvious reluctance to move put a sad edge on the whole proceedings. It seemed such a wrench. However, it also showed how much the Chantlers cared — and that was, in a strange sort of way, most reassuring for Roger and Josie. They would have hated to have bought a house from a couple who did not feel any attachment to the place they were leaving. It wouldn't have been the same. In the end, it was quite a relief when they did actually move in and the Chantlers set off. As they bade farewell to the old couple on their long journey to the other side of the world, Roger and Josie presumed that would be the last they would ever see of them.

So when Wanda turned up on their doorstep some three years later, it came as something of a surprise. She still seemed the same gentle, caring creature they had first met. She explained to them how the move to Australia hadn't worked out. The Hartlands felt genuinely sorry for Wanda. She seemed so distressed by it all. They offered her a friendly cup of tea while she poured out all her problems. All the time they were aware that she seemed to want to say something, but kept straying from the point.

They talked about the woods, the river, the trees, the children, the happy memories. But all it did was make Wanda even more sad. Then she changed the whole course of the conversation.

'Would you sell us back the house. We so dearly want it back.'

The Hartlands were stunned. They entirely understood her sentiments but they told her firmly how happy they were there and that they could not leave it. They felt awful about the whole situation. They could see from Wanda's response that she really had lived in hope of returning to the place of her dreams.

Most people would have respected the Hartland's decision and left it at that but Wanda would not be that easily deterred. It was the only place where she could put her nightmare to rest. She had to have the bungalow back. It was her only chance to lead a normal life again. If she didn't get it the past would haunt her forever.

All her awful visions were returning. It was as if the occupiers had come back to capture and torture her. The Hartlands were becoming like an army of occupation. They were ordering her not to do something. They wanted to stop her from stepping back inside her mental retreat, preventing her from fleeing the evil forces that had plagued her for more than 40 years.

The shock of their refusal to sell the bungalow threw Wanda back into an awful period of her life. It reopened the wounds that all began in 1939...

She was just 17 years old. Her shoulders were broad but perfectly shaped. Her hair was fair and well-conditioned. Her bone structure was strong and her expression was permanently confident. The picture of an attractive girl on the edge of womanhood.

When her father sent her from their home in Western Russia to law school in Berlin, it seemed a natural step for such an exceptionally talented scholar. The first few months there had been a real eye-opener. Being on her own at such a young age had its problems. She overcame them with her looks. They were her passport to a good time. Berlin was a debauched but exciting place in those days. The sense of danger on the streets was always prevalent, but that made it all the more intriguing if you lived there. There were soldiers on every corner but they didn't bother her except to make fresh remarks about her legs. The bars and cafes of Berlin were wonderful. Packed with artists and writers, oblivious to the repressive regime they lived under.

It was an experience of a lifetime for Wanda. She was learning so much. More than she could ever have hoped for back in Russia. And at the end of her three year stay, she would return home as a trained lawyer. It was an achievement that would really mean something to her family. Maybe she could work abroad? That would be even more fun. The world was at her feet. There was so much she could do with her life, so many possible avenues to go down. She could do whatever she wanted. Nobody and nothing could stop her. Or so she thought...

At first, she did not even notice the street violence involving the soldiers with their Swastika armbands. Her mind was focussed on her ambition to succeed. Everything else took second place.

'Outside now!'

The German soldiers did not waste time with explanations.

They were rounding up every name on a list — and Wanda was one of them. She did not know where she was being taken or why. But the look of fear etched on the others' faces told her enough.

They were all students. Young, highly articulate people. None of it made sense. They weren't the enemies of the Germans. They were just studying in Berlin. What was behind all this?

Maybe it was all just a mistake and in a few hours they would be released. But the hours soon turned into days and the days into weeks.

They wanted to know her name, her age, her qualifications. They were particularly interested in her intelligence. They fired question after question at her. How many languages do you speak? What are your qualifications? What is your father's profession? It went on and on and it was becoming very clear that they had something in mind for Wanda. Something awful was about to happen. It would not have been so bad if she knew what it was. The uncertainty was causing the most pain. She was well aware the time would come when they would take her away to some dreadful place.

She thought of escape. But the opportunity never arose.

Soon Wanda was transferred to a prison unlike any she had ever heard about before. It was more like a farm: There were lots of children. Well, very young adults. Nearly all girls. Everyone was relatively free compared to the previous compound. But that very liberty unnerved her. There was something strange about the place. On the surface it seemed like a school in the country or a holiday camp. Underneath, however, you could taste the misery. Students played on the grass in front of the building, but none of them were smiling. And always in the background were the guards with their stiff uniforms and menacing rifles.

All the girls had a certain attractiveness. They had good figures, exquisite faces — and they all shared the same blank look of fear. None of them seemed to know why they were there.

One younger girl — she must have been about 14 — was crying on the shoulders of another. But Wanda didn't know why. It was an uncertainty which would haunt her for the rest of her life.

The guards were young as well, with many still in their teens. Most of them looked typically German: well built, blond hair, big jackboots. It was the real adults who seemed the most terrifying. There were doctors and nurses everywhere bustling around the place.

One day Wanda was subjected to a physical examination the like of which she had never before experienced in her entire life. She thought it was going to be a straightforward medical. It turned out to be an horrific encounter. Something she would never forget.

The doctors examined each of the girls in turn with clinical inquisitiveness. Probing every orifice. The pain when one male doctor roughly examined her made Wanda wince. Then they checked her general health, her strength and fitness. Still Wanda was bemused. Why were all these doctors examining her? What were they planning? She was blissfully unaware that anyone who failed those first medicals went straight to the death camps.

They lived in ignorance for weeks. They were well fed, given many books to read, encouraged to learn and subjected to numerous tests.

Wanda soon realised the doctors were pleased with her. They would say words like 'perfect' and 'beautifully formed' as though they were describing animals rather than human beings.

Then one morning, Wanda was ordered to see the camp's chief physician. She wondered what it was about. She had passed the tests. What more could they possibly want to do to her?

When she walked into the room, there,

standing with the doctor, was a tall, well-built German with blond hair and chiselled features like a cardboard cutout.

He examined Wanda with his sharp crystalline eyes, looking up and down her body as she stood there. At first, they said nothing. She was just ordered to stay still and not speak — just allow this total stranger to cast his eyes all over her body.

The doctor turned to the man and said, 'What do you think.'

That word 'perfect' was used yet again.

It was at last starting to dawn on Wanda why she was there. The doctors. The man. The questions. She was terrified. All the nightmare scenarios she had considered were now coming true.

She had been nurtured and fed at that farm in order to create the perfect baby for the perfect race. She was to become a surrogate mother for the Aryan race — Hitler's consuming obsession.

She was a virgin faced with conveyor belt sex on demand. No emotion. No love.

Wanda was taken into an adjoining room. In the corner was a mattress. She was forced to strip off her clothes...

Forty years later in Pant Perthog, Wanda was reliving that dreadful nightmare. She couldn't get the sex farm out of her mind. Of course, she had thought about it every day for the whole of her life. No one could forget what had happened. But before, she had control over those feelings. Now, she was consumed with out and out anger. The Hartlands were standing in her way. Punishing her. Hadn't she already had punishment enough? She couldn't allow it. She had to do something.

They had become Nazi guards. Their refusal to sell the house was as much an atrocity to her as the behaviour of those blond Aryan brutes.

Wanda's husband Alan was beside himself with worry. He could see his wife's obsession growing at an alarming rate. He tried to explain that there were other places to live. But nowhere except the bungalow would do for Wanda.

The Hartland's would have to suffer for the torture they had inflicted on her.

Wanda's first step was to enroll at the local gun club. The Aberyswyth Rifle Club was the sort of place that is frequented mainly by men. Set in the heart of the Welsh countryside, it was primarily used by genuine enthusists and responsible farmers trying to keep in their aim.

When Wanda first showed up to learn skills with a gun, there were a few raised eyebrows, but the members soon became used to seeing the grandmotherly figure cocking a weapon to her shoulder and firing off round after round of bullets. She rapidly gained a reputation as a very fine shot. No-one asked her why she wanted to learn in the first place. They aren't like that in mid-Wales. Mind your own business, ask no questions and life will stay easy.

Her aim became deadlier by the day.

Josie Hartland was close to tears as she screwed up the letter that had just come through the post box of their house. She was worried by the threats. What made it worse was the fact they both knew exactly who had written it. Wanda Chantler.

It was the third letter to have arrived in a couple of weeks. Each one had become more elaborate. More sinister. And now it mentioned treasure hidden under the bath.

Wanda Chantler was becoming increasingly withdrawn. She and her husband had found a place to live at nearby Garth Owen. But it wasn't the same as the bungalow. The countryside didn't look or sound the same. It was more built up. More noisy. Less private.

Living there made Wanda even more obsessed with moving back to the bungalow. She hated meeting people in the street near their new home. They just didn't seem so friendly.

Wanda felt less and less inclined to go out.

Apart from her trips to the rifle club she rarely left the house. Alan Chantler was becoming increasingly worried about his wife's health and mental state. All she could talk about was the bungalow. How she had to have it back. He kept telling her to forget it. But she would have none of it.

She started to convince herself that she had left some hidden treasure under the bath. A lot of gold trickets and an assortment of other things. Losing the house was bad enough, but the treasure was legally hers. She was the rightful owner. No-one should be allowed to take that away from her. She kept asking the Hartlands, and they said it did not exist. But she knew it was there. She knew it.

Wanda began to write another letter. This time it was to the local paper. The venom soon flowed. Her targets were the Hartlands. If she could not persuade them to give up her house — the house she created and made into what it was today — then she would hound them until they hated the very sight of it.

'You have got to do something. The woman is deranged.'

Roger Hartland had had enough of the threats. His wife was in tears when he had got home that day. It was an outrage that anyone could make such vicious comments about someone they hardly knew.

Something had to be done, so he turned to the police.

Crime was almost non-existent in Pant Perthog. Nothing much ever happened. And that made it all the more difficult for the police to respond rapidly to any problem that might arise. The officers were sympathetic. But how could anyone take a grandmother's threats seriously? There was no possiblity of her carrying them out.

Roger Hartland was convinced otherwise. He believed that Wanda Chantler's threats had the ring of authenticity about them. That was why they were so frightening.

'Just give us a call if you have any more problems.' The policeman was merely doing his duty, but no more. This sort of thing never happened in a place like Pant Perthog, after all. Why should it start now?

Alan Chantler also knew otherwise. He was well aware of Wanda's obsessive nature, after nearly 40 years of marriage. After all, they had first met when he and his fellow allied troops arrived at the sex farm in 1945 and liberated the inhabitants. It was an emotionally draining job. But it had one reward — he met Wanda.

Within a short time, they had married and moved to Britain. Those past horrors seemed to have been put behind them. Wanda never really spoke much about the farm. She bottled it all up, thinking constantly about it but never telling her closest friend. It had to come out sooner or later.

Alan was well aware his wife was on the verge of a nervous breakdown. She had become agrophobic — refusing to leave their new home for anything other than rifle club training.

Reluctantly, he went to the police and got her shotgun licence revoked before any tragedy could occur. Instinctively, he knew she was heading in that direction. He could feel each second ticking away before his wife's inevitable explosion. He was convinced it was only a matter of time before something awful happened. The threats, the letters. She had even been around to the Hartlands to try to frighten them into selling the house.

Wanda's main topic of conversation at home was the treasure under the bath. Alan knew it didn't exist but he also knew that in his wife's mind it was the only piece of reality she could still cling to.

The Hartlands were as bad as the SS in her eyes. Maybe they even came from Germany, she thought. In Wanda's mind, the sex farm and the Hartlands were rapidly becoming synonymous with each other. Maybe they took their orders from the camp commandant? Perhaps they had been sent here to hunt her down and take her back?

One sunny Monday, June 16, 1980, Wanda Chantler plunged into the abyss of insanity.

At Garth Owen, Wanda was in a better mood than she had been for weeks. Alan was delighted by this improvement in his wife's health and decided to leave her for a few hours to do the shopping.

The moment he left the house, she scurried to the wardrobe to get dressed. She felt good inside herself. There was a job to be done. She had an objective for the first time in months. It gave her a fresh appetite for life. Maybe that had been the problem all along? She needed to have something to achieve. Life had to have its goals otherwise what was the point in existing?

Josie Chantler was feeling in the same sort of mood over at Pant Perthog. She was getting on with the household chores like washing and cleaning the kitchen and all the other essential work of the day. She enjoyed keeping the bungalow clean and fresh. The weather made her feel happy as well. It was so rare to get a really nice day in these parts.

The last few weeks had been blissfully clear of problems from that woman. It seemed they had heard the last of her.

Wanda pulled her car up about fifty yards from the entrance to the bungalow, just out of sight of the actual property. She opened the boot, took out two air pistols and tucked them over each hip cowboy fashion.

Then she lifted out the double barrelled shotgun. It was much heavier than the pistols. But then it was also far more lethal.

Lastly, she took out that treasured painting of the landscape surrounding the bungalow — one of the pictures she had toiled over so lovingly all those years before.

She looked an incongruous sight with the thick leather belt strapped around her waist over a very tweedy, country outfit. If it were not for the guns, she would have looked like a typical country squire's wife out for a walk in the country.

It was quite difficult to carry the shotgun and the painting. But Wanda managed. The determination was there. She could achieve anything that day.

She had to get away from the Nazis. Get them out of her life for ever. Destroy them before they destroyed her.

As she walked up to the front door, her mind kept flashing back to the sex farm. The experiments, the examinations, the clinical rape. This time she would rid herself of those memories once and for all. She would have her revenge. And her treasure under the bath. And her bungalow.

She thought she was back in Germany. It all seemed so clear.

'I have a present for you.'

The Hartlands were stunned when they opened the front door to see Wanda standing, armed like some sort of elderly, female Rambo, on the step.

'It's a painting I did of the area. I thought you would like it.'

'You've got to come quickly. She's got three guns... The Hartlands' telephone call to Alan Chantler was still remarkably calm, considering the arsenal of weapons she had on her.

She waited on the doorstep.

Roger Hartland went to open the front door to tell her that Mr Chantler was on his way. Wanda aimed the shotgun straight at the entrance. As it opened, Roger saw the barrel pointing right at him for a split second before it went off.

The sheer force of the shot sent him to the ground in a crumpled heap.

Inside, Josie Hartland was grappling for the phone. Dialing 999. She just hoped the operator would answer quickly. She got through, but was told to wait for a police officer to come on the line. Seconds passed while she waited for the answer. Still there was no-one at the other end of the line. When would they come? Hurry. Hurry. Hurry.

Wanda was now in the bungalow, seeking out her tormentors. She entered the kitchen quietly to see Josie cowering in a corner of the room with the phone, frantically shouting down the receiver in the desperate hope someone would help her.

But all she had in fact done was lead Wanda to her. Wanda stood for a moment and stared at Josie before cocking her gun.

The two shots hit her full on. But she was still alive. Still struggling for breath.

Wanda calmly reloaded the shotgun and fired another shot. One was enough to finish off the enemy. They were so weak when you confronted them. Cowards squirming pathetically in a corner. She hadn't even used up all her rounds.

On 24 October, 1980, Wanda Chantler admitted the manslaughter of the Hartlands and was sent to Broadmoor Hospital without limit of time. Sentencing her, Mr Justice Hodgson said: 'Nobody could possibly have heard what we have here without feeling the most terrible compassion. In a sense, you are as much a victim of your Nazi experiences as the Hartlands were victims of that same horror.'

Blood Beach

Santa Barbara, California, is one of those beachside paradises most people can only dream about. Miles and miles of pure white sand overlooking the Pacific Ocean. A picturesque seafront town with a scattering of bars and restaurants attractively designed to guarantee hundreds of thousands of visitors each summer. Immaculately clean pavements and streets kept pristine by a city council that insists on nothing but the best. And famous in Britain as the setting for possibly the worst soap opera ever written.

Yet Santa Barbara is situated just two hours' drive north of the sprawling metropolis of Los Angeles and all its well-publicised problems. That means the local police are always on the lookout for troublemakers entering their little piece of heaven-by-the-sea. Santa Barbara is primarily known as a family-orientated town but beneath that wholesome exterior lies a seedy underbelly typical of any seaside community from Brighton to Benidorm.

And, according to many locals, the 'distasteful' elements included the notorious El Capitan beach just outside town. For this was where the home values and strait-laced beliefs of so much of Middle America were thrown out of the window. In a country where bare breasts are censored on prime-time television yet mass killings are considered fair game, the El Capitan beach was a place that people only referred to in hushed tones. You see, it was a good, old-fashioned nudist beach.

Lots of nature lovers would saunter down to the isolated beauty spot and strip off in a desperate bid for that famous all-over tan. Interestingly, the majority of visitors to El Capitan were middle-aged. Youngsters seemed to avoid the place like the plague. It must have been their puritanical upbringing that did it. Remember, more than seventy per cent of America's population still go to church every Sunday!

Phillip Bogdanoff and his pretty wife Diana were two such avid sun worshippers. They loved making the short trip from their mobile home at El Capitan Beach Ranch Park, which overlooked the sea. In fact, it was a dream come true for Phillip. He had a healthy — some people would say unhealthy — interest in examining the figures of all those nude beachgoers. He was always subtly casting his gaze across the perfectly formed muscles and firm thighs of some of the beach's other, more fanatical, visitors.

The handsome, rugged, fun-loving 49-year-old engineer kept himself in pretty good shape, too. He was extremely proud of his body and relished the chance to strip off completely. He had been a regular at the beach for many years when he met attractive fair-haired Diana in nearby Colefax, California. She was working as a nursing aide at a nearby convalescent hospital when they met in 1984. A four-year courtship followed, during which they learned just about everything there was to know about each other. Both had suffered broken marriages, so they were understandably cautious at first. In any case, Diana already had children from her previous husband, so there was no hurry to tie the knot.

Eventually, in February, 1989, they married and moved to their dream location right opposite the most infamous beach in Santa Barbara. And whenever they were not working during that summer, Diana and Phillip loved to pack a towel and set off on the short walk down to El Capitan.

Phillip had been so relieved when Diana voiced absolutely no objections to stripping off in a public place. He even had a sneaking suspicion that she rather enjoyed exhibiting her body to the beach population that tended to consist of rather more men than women. Sometimes Phillip would catch healthily endowed guys staring at his wife's pert body and smile at them, before they could avert their gaze in embarrassment at being 'caught' peeping.

Diana, for her part, would sometimes sneakily open her legs just a fraction if she knew some of the more handsome specimens were watching at her eye-level. She got a thrill out of letting them see just a hint. Phillip seemed to know precisely what his wife was playing at and he gave it his own bizarre seal of approval by just observing — and enjoying — the proceedings.

Their other favourite pastime was frolicking in the warm ocean. They both agreed that nude swimming was a hell of a refreshing way to pass the time. Diana and Phillip loved that feeling when the water rushed past them, sending surf crashing all over their skin. They used to say it was second only to making love.

But, back on the beach during those swelteringly hot summer months of 1989, Diana often used to let her mind wander to other, less innocent, things as she sunbathed. She would close her eyes in the bright sunlight and think about... those passionate sex sessions with the manager of the trailer park.

She ran her tongue down his neck and over his right nipple before biting gently into his soft skin. Then she moved back to his mouth and started probing deeply with her tongue. Running the tip right across his gums, flicking it rapidly back and forth.

Then she opened her own mouth as wide as possible so that he could plunge his tongue halfway down her throat. The passion between them was endless. Diana Bogdanoff did not once consider her new husband, lying on the nudist beach just a few hundred yards away.

She had only met the man a few days earlier when he helped them move into their new home. But he caught her looking him up and down and knew they would end up in bed together.

Now, Diana was enjoying what she liked doing best — making hot, steamy love with a rampant male. Naturally, she was on top most of the time. She loved to tease and tantalise them. Make them come really close to climaxing then let go for a split second. It always made them beg for more.

The irony was that her husband of just a few months was on that nearby nudist beach ogling at naked bodies, probably in a highly excitable state. But she preferred to relax another man's tension.

Back in the trailer that day, she was giving the park manager the sort of servicing he had previously only dreamed about. She was willing and prepared to do anything to please him, just so long as she stayed in charge. As they lay there, hot and sweaty after hours of love-making, she sat up and looked through the window at that notorious beach across the street and smiled to herself. Her husband got his pleasure watching naked bodies. She got her enjoyment from performing the real thing. It made her realise that her marriage was a sham — something she should never have gotten herself into. She started thinking of a way out of it.

'If you wanted to kill someone, how would you do it?' Her secret lover thought he was hearing things. Did she really just suggest she wanted to kill someone, moments after enjoying sex?

'Come on. A guy like you must know how it can be done.'

Still he did not reply. The sex between them may well have been out of this world but when she started talking about murdering her husband he began to wonder what sort of relationship he had got himself involved in.

Diana was not deterred by his reluctance to reply. Her mind was set on that particular subject. There was no two ways about it. She was trying to devise a way to kill her husband.

'I thought about lacing his food with cocaine. D'you think that might work?'

'I doubt it. He'd probably just end up getting high and havin' a great time.'

'What about poison? What d'you reckon would be the best brand to use?'

Her illicit lover could hardly believe his ears. Here he was, enjoying a highly charged, sexual affair with an attractive 40-year-old woman and all she wanted to talk about was how to murder her husband!

So he played along with her 'game'. She could not possibly be serious.

'You wanna try getting some of that poison from those pencil trees that grow out near Morro Bay.'

He could not believe he had just said that. Now he was starting to encourage her to do it. He stopped in his tracks. Enough was enough.

'Hey, that's a great idea. Will you come with me and help me find some of those trees?'

Her secret mobile-home lover shook his head vehemently.

'No way. You must be crazy. Forget it. Get a divorce if you're so unhappy.'

Diana got out of bed in a sulky silence, put her

clothes on and headed out of the one and only door to that trailer. She was furious that he would not help her. She would have to find someone else to help hatch her callous plan.

'He's beaten me and abused me more than I can handle. I gotta do something.'

Diana Bogdanoff was pretty convincing as a battered wife, especially when the person she was appealing to was her stunningly attractive 18-year-old daughter Stephanie. The gorgeous dark-haired teenager sat rivetted by her mother's appalling revelations. How could her step-father be such a beast?

'You gotta help me kill him. It's the only way.'

'But, mom. That's murder you're talkin' about. Just get away from him. Just leave him.'

'But I've got nothing. If I leave him I'll be out on the streets. If we kill him, at least I'll get to keep the house and all our money and things.'

'You're crazy!'

Like any self-respecting daughter, Stephanie was genuinely worried about her mother's safety at the hands of her allegedly brutal husband. She feared for her safety, but to murder him did seem rather drastic. However, Diana Bogdanoff could sense her daughter's misplaced sympathy beginning to grow. She gave up her first attempt to organise the killing but there would be other opportunities.

At least three more times, Diana called up her daughter at her home fifty miles away in Bakersfield and begged her to help her end her husband's life.

On the first two occasions she got the same reply — a definite 'No way'. But on the third attempt, Stephanie took heed of the real panic in her mother's voice and she gave in.

'I know this isn't right but if it's the only way then I guess we'll have to do it.'

Diana Bogdanoff was so happy. The longer she spent with Phillip, the more she realised how much she despised him. The only time when she did not feel such a deep hatred for him was when they lay on that nudist beach surrounded by bare bodies, and she would close her eyes and part her legs ever so slightly and start to think back to her passionate interludes with other men.

Stephanie was in overall charge of their mission and she chose her long-time admirer Raymond Stock to carry out the execution. He was so besotted with the shapely, long-legged teenager that he was prepared to sacrifice his liberty for her.

'There isn't anything I wouldn't do for you,' Stock told Stephanie when she put her mother's extraordinary request to him.

But his love obsession for her was somewhat

sweetened by the promise of $10,000 and part-ownership of a house.

As the stunning-looking Stephanie snuggled up close to Stock on the settee at his home, she playfully stroked his thigh and said: 'I promise we'll be together afterwards and I'll give you the time of your life.'

The scene was set. Now the besotted lover had to go out and prove he really was the man of her dreams.

Within hours they had stolen a car, switched its number plates and pointed the bumper in the direction of Santa Barbara. As they drove the one-hour trip, they talked in vivid detail about the plan to murder Phillip Bogdanoff.

It was pretty simple really. Go to his mobile home, wait for him to open the door and pump him full of bullets. But Stock started to get an uneasy feeling as Stephanie clinically talked her way through every move. He had a sick kind of feeling in his stomach. As they approached the outskirts of Santa Barbara, his conscience got the better of him. The idea of blasting Phillip Bogdanoff to death seemed all wrong. His hands were shaking. Even with Stephanie snuggled close to him as they drove, kissing and licking his ears, neck and cheeks throughout the journey. There was no way he could do it. The same thought kept going through Stock's mind: 'I'll go to hell if I do this.'

When he told Stephanie he was pulling out of it,

she was surprisingly calm. They turned the car around and headed back to Bakersfield in total silence. When he dropped her off at her home, she had already decided that she would never see Stock again. He had just paid the ultimate price for not carrying out what he had promised.

Within a few days, though, Stephanie had enticed another of the men so besotted with her. This time his name was Danny Kaplan, another neighbour from Bakersfield. He said later that there was something incredibly alluring about the teenager. When she nuzzled up to him and said she needed a favour, he couldn't wait to help. Even after she had explained the task at hand, he took a big gulp and decided to carry out the dirty deed, all in the name of love.

'I loved her so much I'd have done anything for her,' said Kaplan later. It was a familiar story. Stephanie had that sort of effect on men.

He did not even object when Stephanie said her regular boyfriend, 21-year-old Brian Stafford, would be accompanying them on their quest for murder. Kaplan's love for her was so strong he would have put up with anything. He really believed he would be her only true love in the end.

A few days after that, they both loaded shotguns and rifles into Kaplan's car and headed back towards Santa Barbara. This time the plan was to blast Phillip

Bogdanoff to death as he drove alongside them on the motorway on his way back home from work.

By the time they arrived near the office where he worked, all three were pretty hyped up about what was about to happen. They sat in a discreet vantage point overlooking the main entrance to the building and waited for Bogdanoff to come out.

Hours passed by and still there was no sign of him leaving the office. Soon, darkness fell and the three accomplices began to realise that maybe he was not even there. They started to get agitated. And Kaplan began to wonder what on earth he was doing there in the first place.

'Let's call it a day. We'll have to think up a different way to do this.'

Stephanie, as usual, was very much in charge. As the two men bundled their mini-armoury of weapons back into the boot of the car, she began trying to work out a different way of killing her 'evil' step-father. But all those hours of waiting had a different kind of effect on Kaplan.

'I'm not going through with it. I can't do it.'

Stephanie and her boyfriend Brian Stafford were astonished by Kaplan's outburst. Here they all were about to assassinate a man and one member of the hit team was getting cold feet.

'Come on. You promised. We all agreed.'

Stephanie made it sound more like a playground

dare than a mission to murder.

'No way. I cannot murder an innocent man.'

'But he's not innocent. He's beaten my mom. He deserves to die.'

'You don't know that for sure.'

Stephanie tried in vain to persuade Kaplan to the contrary, but it was no good. They had lost a crucial team player. They would have to go back to the drawing board yet again.

But nothing would stop Stephanie from going ahead with it in the end. She just would not give up. All the ominous signs were clearly there. But she ignored them all out of a fierce loyalty for her 'battered' mother. The right opportunity would come along eventually.

And boyfriend Stafford was still as passionate about Stephanie as ever. He would do anything for her, in exchange for the romance he so desperately wanted to keep going.

Just a few weeks later on September 21 1989, Stephanie, Stafford and his great pal Ricky Rogers teamed up for what they hoped would be a third-time-lucky bid to murder Phillip Bogdanoff.

On this occasion, the plan had changed somewhat. The two men were going to head for the Bogdanoffs' favourite beach at El Capitan.

That day had started off perfectly normally for Diana and Phillip Bogdanoff. The hot September sun had, not surprisingly, enticed the couple out onto the beach, where they could not resist stripping off all their clothes and trying to top up their all-over tans.

El Capitan was pretty busy that day. The surf was crashing down, forming huge slicks of bubbly froth on the sand as dozens of sunworshippers lay completely naked on their specially reserved strip of beach.

Diana and Phillip took up their favourite spot just a few yards from the water's edge. It was the perfect location for him to cast his eyes across the beautiful oiled bodies soaking up the sunshine. Diana was a little more tetchy than usual. She found it difficult to lie still. But then there was rather a lot on her mind that day.

Instead of laying flat on her back as she normally did, Diana found herself sitting up with her knees close to her breasts as she watched the crowds from a distance. Watching. Waiting. Watching. Waiting.

When Phillip looked up, he noticed his wife's behaviour but simply took it as further evidence that she was coming around to his way of thinking. Bodies were beautiful to look at. It never once crossed his mind that she was actually looking out for two particularly over-covered bodies.

The trouble was the more she looked out for her

accomplices, the more she found herself ogling the naked men stretched out in the immediate vicinity. She got quite embarrassed when one guy started trying to give her the come on because she had been gazing past his right shoulder at two men loitering near the beach wall.

She only looked away when they came close enough for her to see that they were the very people she had been waiting for. Reassured that her command was finally about to be carried out, she lay on her back and relaxed. A warm smile was all she was wearing as she lay there and started to fantasise about life without him. It was 11am and there were only a few minutes left of Phillip Bogdanoff's life.

'Hey, man. You gotta joint?'

The two men were standing right over the naked figures of Diana and Phillip Bogdanoff, blocking the sun from carrying out its duty to give them that essential all-over tan.

'I'm sorry. What did you say?'

Phillip was not even sure he had heard them right.

'I said: You got some grass?'

Phillip was more a martini type of character. Cannabis had never been on his social menu.

'I don't smoke.'

He was nervous of these two men. There was

something about them. They seemed to be preparing to do something, but Phillip Bogdanoff did not know what. Diana did not move. She lay there saying nothing.

Just then, the two men looked at each other nervously. The quiet one pulled a pistol and pointed it straight at Bogdanoff in silence and pulled the trigger.

The bullet ripped through his cheek, spinning him off balance. That first wound was neat but ineffective. Brian Stafford moved even nearer to his victim and fired again. This time Phillip Bogdanoff's head recoiled and he slumped to the ground.

'All I wanted to do was stop his pain,' said Brian Stafford later when trying to justify why he fired that second shot.

Back on the beach that day, Diana Bogdanoff screamed in terror. She might have set the whole thing up but the reality of the murder was still enough to spark off her emotions. The most horrifying evidence of the killing was her husband's blood splattered all over her naked breasts and stomach. She looked down at herself and shrieked.

Gunman Stafford coolly and calmly put his pistol back inside his shirt and started to disappear down the beach with his accomplice. Their mission had been completed. They heard her cries for help and looked around for a moment and saw her kneeling, naked and bloody, over the corpse of her husband — the man she had ordered them to kill.

Within minutes the secluded calm of that naturists' paradise had been cruelly destroyed by hundreds of police, paramedics, coroners' officers, press and onlookers desperately trying to get a glimpse of the grisly sight of a naked guy blasted to bits on the beach in front of his wife.

Just a few yards from where her husband had been killed, sat the shaking figure of Diana Bogdanoff. Wearing a pullover to cover her blood — splattered skin, the hysterical widow was being comforted by a tourist who just happened to be walking by moments after the shooting and had immediately offered her his jumper for cover.

'They shot my husband. They shot my husband.'

She just kept repeating the words over and over again. It was an impressive performance. The truth is that she probably did feel bereaved and shocked in a weird way, because talking about murder is a whole lot different from going through with it.

Through rivers of tears, Diana told police of the two complete strangers who came up to her husband and ended his life just because he told them he did not smoke pot.

'Phillip didn't do anything,' she weeped. 'He didn't say anything to make them angry. He was just sitting there.'

Detectives were baffled and they all said how

sorry they felt for that poor, grieving widow.

'It seemed a senseless cruel killing,' said one cop on the TV news that night. The town of Santa Barbara was under a state of siege by the media, and some residents genuinely feared that the mystery killers might strike again at any time and any place.

But the only place Brian Stafford and his friend Ricky Rogers were heading was back to their homes in Bakersfield, with the beautiful Stephanie alongside them in the car.

As far as she was concerned, this was a time to celebrate. She had helped her poor, battered mother get out of a nightmare marriage to a monster. And Diana would still have a home to live in and a good income from his life insurance.

When the murdering threesome arrived back at Stephanie's home she broke open a few beers and proposed a toast.

'To a job well done.'

The beer bottles clinked in unison. Their mission had been accomplished.

Then they switched on the television and found exactly what they were looking for. A suitably distressed Diana Bogdanoff pouring out her heart and soul to the TV news cameras as she played an Oscar-winning role as the tragic widow. She shed more tears, wrung her hands and gave a wonderfully convincing performance.

The three killers looked on and laughed. It had all gone so smoothly they could hardly believe it had really happened.

Within a few minutes Ricky Rogers had left, and Stephanie climbed into bed with her athletic lover and switched her attention to a pastime her mother would definitely have approved of.

Detectives Russ Birchim and Fred Ray were seasoned homicide cops who had investigated just about every type of murder over the years. But the slaying in cold blood of Phillip Bogdanoff truly baffled them.

As one of them said: 'No-one gets killed over a joint. Certainly not in a nudist beach in broad daylight.'

There was only one conclusion as far as they were concerned: Bogdanoff's wife had something to do with it.

But Diana was not about to throw away her entire life by confessing to a crime she knew they could not pin on her. She stuck rigidly to her story about the 'tragic' death of her loving husband.

Neighbours at the El Capitan Ranch Park had only good things to say about the Bogdanoffs. 'Nice couple.' 'Kept themselves to themselves.' 'A sweet pair.' They could do no wrong in the eyes of those who knew them.

Detectives Birchim and Ray plugged away with composite sketches of the two killers based on eye-witnesses' reports. Hundreds of likely-looking suspects were pulled in, interrogated and cleared. The investigation went on like that for a month.

Birchim and Ray chewed over a few other possible theories. Maybe the two gunmen were a couple of screwballs who were high on dope? Perhaps it was all a case of mistaken identity?

But, whatever their suspicions about the case, there was no hard and fast evidence to go on. The two cops were swimming around in the dark.

Then an anonymous caller phoned in to a police informants' hotline in Bakersfield. The man said he had information about the nude beach murder in Santa Barbara.

'I thought they were joking,' he told the police operator. 'Then I saw the newspaper reports and realised they had done it.'

The tipster then told the operator the names of the people he claimed were involved. The first one on his list was Raymond Stock, the man who had been involved in the initial abortive attempt on the life of Phillip Bogdanoff.

When detectives called at his home in Bakersfield he confessed that he had almost killed Bogdanoff.

The next one on the list was Danny Kaplan. He

had a similar story to tell. But this time he furnished the police with the names of Stafford and his pal Ricky Rogers, as well as ringleader Stephame.

Kaplan even told officers how Stafford, Rogers and Stephanie came back to her apartment after the actual killing, bragging about what they had just done.

'They were saying: "We did it. We did it. We blew the sucker away." '

Kaplan had sat there listening to them with a sinking feeling in his stomach. He knew full well who they were talking about.

Within days, the gang of assassins had been rounded up and by the time Diana Bogdanoff returned from a trip to visit relatives in Washington state, the police were there at the airport to greet her.

For months she stuck rigidly to her story that she was innocent of any involvement in her husband's death. Then her first husband came forward and revealed that when the couple had divorced in 1980, she had told him:

'You're lucky you're still alive. I tried to hire two men to kill you.'

For Diana Bogdanoff, killing lovers and husbands had been an obsession for years. It just took the perfect opportunity for her to realise her lifetime ambition.

In March, 1991, at the Santa Barbara County Superior

Court, Stephanie pleaded guilty to second-degree murder and received a fifteen-year-to-life sentence. Boyfriend Brian Stafford pleaded guilty to first-degree murder and got thirty-three years after agreeing to testify against Diana Bogdanoff. In June, 1991, Ricky Rogers entered a plea of no contest to one charge of voluntary manslaughter. He was sentenced to no more than ten years in jail because he did not pull the trigger.

Meanwhile, in October, 1990, Diana Bogdanoff went on trial at the same courthouse. After hours of deliberation, the judge pronounced a mis-trial because the jury could not agree on a verdict. At her second trial in May, 1991, jurors took just two hours to find her guilty of first-degree murder. She was also found guilty of planning the murder for financial gain and lying in wait for the killing to take place. Under those 'special circumstances', she was given an automatic life sentence without parole.

A Marriage Made in Hell

Her face was vibrant. Neat, smooth features somehow made even more attractive by the straight bridge of her Roman nose. Then there were her eyes. Dark seas of diamonds. Glistening with an intriguing combination of vitality and animal cunning. When she looked at people, the lids would narrow slightly. They held a magnetism that was almost hypnotic. Even her long, flowing dark hair was eye-catching as the neon lights bounced off her head like a sun setting behind a mountain.

Then there were her breasts. Firm, ample, shapely. Pointing straight ahead so as to catch the eye of any passing admirer. They clung to the silky blouse that was undone just enough to reveal a hint of bosom. Her bottom was just as well designed. A definite curve, yet still retaining the delicate look that made men want to pat it ever so gently. Her legs were covered in black stockings that night, the skirt began two inches above the knee. They hinted at her sexuality, but not so much that it might put any man off the goods on offer. Her whole appearance was geared around her persona — sultry, sexual and very, very luscious.

William Nelson was transfixed by her as she stood at the bar of a small tavern in Costa Mesa, California, that evening in the winter of 1991. He did not know her name or anything about her, but he could not keep his eyes off her. Every now and again she turned and smiled ever so slightly. But he could not be sure if it was a come- on or wishful thinking on his part. In any case, what would a truly beautiful 23-year-old woman be doing trying to tempt a haggard 56-year-old? No, thought William, it must be my imagination. He returned to his beer, delighted to be enjoying his liberty again after just being released from a long spell inside.

William could not get that girl out of his mind.

Every time he looked up she was still there, gazing over in his direction. He tried to avert his eyes, watch the other people in the bar. Next to him, three bikers were discussing the inner workings of their Harley Davidsons. Over at the other end of the bar, a couple seemed deeply engrossed in some emotional upheaval or other. Across the way, three gaudy girls giggled and laughed and caught his eye the instant he looked in their direction. William looked away hastily; he had seen two of those women on a lot of occasions before in that bar and he knew they were definitely the types to avoid. Two of them had their own slinky dress code that consisted of stone-washed skin-tight jeans and razor-sharp stilettos. On that particular night, the other one — a strawberry blonde — had on a black and white checked pair of hotpants that were so short and so tight you could see the seam of her tights, as well as the separated cheeks of her bottom. William knew that, however desperate he might be for a woman, those three were to be avoided.

Then his eyes panned around once more in the direction of that mystery girl, sitting all alone at the bar. This time she had crossed her legs as she sat on a stool. It had the desirable effect of hitching up her skirt a further three, or maybe even four, inches to reveal a full pair of thighs that were very much enhanced by their covering of black stocking. William could just make out the seams of those stockings as they travelled from her neat, trim ankles up and up into the shadow above her thighs that old men could only dream about.

This time he looked up and definitely caught a look of recognition. There was no doubting it. William felt a shiver of expectation run through his body. She was a very attractive woman and she seemed interested in him...

Omaima Stainbrook was well aware of the probing, lusting eyes of William Nelson feasting upon her very trim body as she sat at that bar. But she never liked to hurry herself. She knew full well that if she made it too easy for him then he might just take her for a prostitute, and she was looking for a long-term relationship not some cheap and nasty sex followed by an instant dismissal.

Omaima was just 23 years old, but she had already led a pretty full life. She knew exactly how to tempt and titillate men, and William was about to join a long list of useful admirers.

But before she even talked to him, she wanted to tease and tantalise him some more. She swung her stool around a few inches, so that she was virtually facing him, and took a long drag of her cigarette before opening her legs just a fraction. She could feel his eyes longing for her now. It was a good feeling. She always enjoyed those first few minutes when the hunt was in its preliminary stages. There was something very exciting about knowing that a complete stranger was lusting after you. But then Omaima was looking for something much more than a mere tease.

She pulled her lipstick out of her handbag and pressed it firmly against the edge of her mouth. With her mirror in one hand and the lipstick in the other, she wiped the stick across and then back over her lips. Slowly, ever so slowly, she held the rounded end of the lipstick to her lips for a moment and glanced casually in William Nelson's direction. She smiled as their eyes caught each other.

Within seconds, the lipstick was back in the handbag and William Nelson was making his first tentative effort to approach this beautiful creature of the night.

'Hi. Would you like a drink?'

William did not know what else to say. He might have spent quite a few years in jail, but he was not some hardened criminal. His offences were things like smuggling electronic goods into Mexico, and the odd bit of dope. Throughout all his jail terms, he had always retained a truly gentlemanly manner — and that night was no exception.

'No. I've got one, thanks.'

Omaima was not going to make it that easy for William. She wanted him to make a real effort to catch her, then she would know that he was serious and not some married man out to get an easy lay.

She took out a cigarette and put it to her lips slowly, almost sensuously, and waited. At first, William was so nervous he did not think to offer her a light. Then she parted two fingers and put them up to the filter. Suddenly it clicked.

William grappled for his lighter and, almost shaking with excitement, held it just steady enough to ignite her cigarette.

'Thanks.'

She purred the word in such a way that William knew it was now or never. He had to start up a conversation before the silence killed off her lust for him instantly.

Within a few minutes they were sharing drinks and laughter as he told her about himself, neatly avoiding the obvious questions about being married and material wealth. Ironically, they were the two subjects dearest to Omaima's heart.

But she was not deterred. William was well dressed. He had a certain poise and confidence and he was wearing plenty of gold jewellery. Omaima reckoned she might be onto a good thing with William Nelson, and he certainly had no idea of the risks he was taking by even considering her as a partner.

Only a year earlier, Huntington Beach resident Robert Hanson had found himself embroiled with Omaima

Stambrook after a very similar encounter. The middle-aged clerk was clearly enchanted and flattered by the attentions of the beautiful young Egyptian-born immigrant and within a few weeks of meeting they had moved in together to his luxury apartment just near the Pacific Ocean.

It was a dream come true for Omaima. The sort of home that she could never have dreamt of owning all those years earlier when she was virtually destitute and living on the streets of Cairo.

Now she was engaged to be married to an elderly Californian who would ensure that she never had to return to that awful life that drove her into the arms of Mother America in the first place. The United States is the place of dreams for millions of people around the world, but for Omaima it was now a reality and she was determined to have herself the best life possible. But without a job, the only way to that fantasy world was with the help of men. She had discovered at an early age that her striking beauty could get her places. Men would literally fall at her feet. They would do anything for her.

Robert Hanson was just one such man in a long line of elderly males that Omaima tempted. She had learnt a long time ago that she was capable of doing anything to get what she wanted.

But when Robert had refused to marry Omaima it sparked off a fury inside her that was virtually uncontainable. Her only purpose in sleeping with Robert and moving into his house was to get him to marry her. Then she knew she was guaranteed an income for life. It was her way of ensuring she never had to return to the streets of Cairo again.

When he told her that he could not possibly marry her, despite the fact they had been living together for some months, she went crazy with anger. The feeling of betrayal built up so quickly within her that she could hardly stop herself shaking with rage. And when Robert Hanson returned one evening from a hard day at the office, she pulled a knife on him and locked him in the bedroom while she rifled through his wallet for all the money she could find. She knew it was time to leave him because her plan had failed. But first she wanted to get what she believed was rightfully hers. When she could find only a few dollars in loose change, Omaima got even crazier and went after her live-in lover with the knife. He survived the attack and, too embarrassed at first to report it to the police, allowed Omaima to leave quietly.

Meanwhile she had sworn never to let any man sleep with her until they were married. That way, she wouldn't have that same problem ever again.

Now, back in that bar in Costa Mesa, she was about to ensnare another middle-aged man. But this time she would not waste her time living with him. This was marriage or nothing. But even Omaima knew that if she pushed for marriage within a few minutes of meeting William Nelson in that bar, it might scare him off. Instead, she allowed his hand to travel up that shapely thigh of hers as they sat together and just smiled a warm sensuous smile that convinced William that he was onto something good. But then the ex-convict had a few secrets of his own. And he was already so besotted by this dark-haired beauty that he did not give them even a moment's consideration as they stared into each other's eyes.

'What can you possibly see in me?'

It seemed a perfectly reasonable question for an ageing man to ask a shapely young temptress. Omaima blushed heavily and ran her hand gently up the inside of his trouser leg before digging her long nails into his flesh.

'You're so strong, William. I need your strength to guide me through life.'

Unfortunately, William Nelson interpreted Omaima's words as a plea from the heart. The truth was that she was doing the devil's work and she still had a long way to go before she achieved her goal.

As he leant against her firm breasts and kissed her full, luscious glossy lips, all he could feel was the moisture of her tongue as it returned his gesture. He felt sure he could feel the electricity between them instantly.

Omaima allowed her tongue to probe the inner workings of his mouth without even giving it much consideration. An initial French kiss was but a small price to pay to entrap William Nelson in her weird world. The next stage might prove altogether more difficult.

Omaima's eyes positively lit up when he gave her a lift home in his gleaming red Corvette sports car. She had long since picked up that American habit of judging people by the car they drove, and William Nelson had just passed with flying colours.

She sat back and felt the warm November wind flow through her hair as he accelerated out of the parking lot with that powerful V8 engine virtually at full thrust. She would let him drop her off at her place and just allow him a goodnight kiss — nothing more at this early stage. She certainly didn't want to appear to be an easy lay. She just wanted to let him know she was interested. That would be enough to have the desired effect.

'But I cannot sleep in the same bed as you unless we are married.'

Omaima was most insistent. William Nelson might have been smitten by this beautiful woman, but he was expecting to have sex with her by the time they had been out on their third date. She had other plans.

'It is against my religious beliefs. I just cannot do

it.' William was disappointed but not deterred. He had known Omaima just a few days but he had felt they were getting so close that making love together seemed only natural. He had suppressed his sexual appetite for long enough whilst in jail. Now, he had been out a few months, and he planned to take every opportunity that came his way.

'But here in the States it doesn't matter.'

'It might not matter to you, William, but I still have very strong beliefs. I must stick to them.'

William looked at his girlfriend and smiled. She was positively oozing with sensuality even as they sat there on the couch in his flat, talking. He had hardly been able to take his eyes off her since the first moment they met. He had even fantasised about what he wanted to do to her, as he lay in bed alone after that first meeting. He had memorised every inch of her body. He had imagined all the things they would do together. But now he was faced with the reality of the situation. She was saying they could not sleep together unless they were married. He knew he could not marry her. For a start, it seemed crazy to wed a girl just a few days after meeting — and then there was Katherine, over in Santa Maria, just fifty miles away. She might not be too pleased about it. After all, she was still his wife.

William was in a dilemma. He wanted this gorgeous young thing so badly that he would do anything to have her. He had never felt so tempted by a woman in all his life. He put his hands around her trim waist as they stood there in the hallway of his flat and hugged her tight. So tightly, in fact, that he did not feel the stiff tension running through her body. She only began to relax a little when he talked.

'Well, I must be crazy but I don't think I can live without you. Will you marry me?'

William Nelson did not know what had come over him. But he just had to have her.

Omaima did not even bother to reply. She just nodded her head and buried her face in his chest, smiling ever so discreetly to herself as she felt his hand travel up the back of her tight-fitting skirt. In the space of just a few days she had achieved precisely what she set out to do.

The wedding was a simple affair as marriages go. But then Omaima did not mind. She just looked down at that certificate and breathed a huge sigh of relief. It had taken her just seven days from the moment she first met William Nelson. She looked over at the slightly crumpled figure of the 56-year-old man she had just agreed to make her husband and realised that marriage was a very small sacrifice to make, under the circumstances. She was certain he had some money and a visible means of supporting her. Now the whole scene was set.

She had fixed herself firmly into a position where

a man was supporting her and would continue to do so for the rest of her life. As they boarded a plane on the afternoon of their wedding to go on honeymoon to Laredo, Texas, she was feeling very pleased with herself.

But William Nelson had other things on his mind during that trip. It was supposed to be the ultimate confirmation of their love for one another and, on that first night, William was indeed delighted when he finally got to sleep with Omaima. The sex might have been a little one-sided but she still looked sensational as she lay there waiting for him to join her in their hotel bed.

As he feasted on every inch of her body, she returned his passion vaguely. She was more excited by the thought of that nice apartment back in Costa Mesa and how she was going to completely redecorate it when they got back after the honeymoon. William did not really notice that his new wife's mind was on other things. The act of sex was a great way to escape the worries of the world for a few lustful minutes, and that was the way William looked at it. The business pressures were mounting and even the trip to Laredo had an ulterior purpose.

The Texas city's busy little airport had become the epicentre of his smuggling empire. It was just a short hop into Mexico, and William had become one of the most powerful smugglers of cheap electrical goods into the Central American nation that has always craved products of every size and shape from its fabulously wealthy neighbour — the US.

The trouble was that his lucrative business had been neglected during his most recent spell in prison and he needed desperately to build up the smuggling operation once more. That meant meetings with shady characters on isolated stretches of desert. It also meant leaving Omaima alone at their hotel for huge chunks of their honeymoon.

Still, at least she knew he was in business. Even if she did not realise just how illicit his work was. But all those long lonely hours at the hotel did enable Omaima to search through her brand new husband's belongings to find out more about him. With all the secrets she hid, it was only natural that she should suspect the man she had entrapped of having a few of his own.

But what she eventually found made her even madder than Robert Hanson had when he refused to marry her the previous year in Huntington Beach.

Omaima could not quite believe her eyes when she looked at the snapshot she had found in her new husband's jacket pocket. He was posing happily with a motherly-looking woman in her forties. It was clearly taken in recent months. He even had on the same shirt he had been wearing that first night they met in the Costa Mesa bar. But the most insulting thing was that he looked so happy.

She knew instinctively that this had to be someone very special in William's life. There was something about their closeness in that photograph that gave it all away. His arm was around this other woman, holding her tight. If Omaima's worst fears were confirmed, then her whole marriage scheme might have been a complete waste of time. Her intention had been to lure William into a relationship that was legally signed and sealed so that she was financially secure for life.

She tried to stop herself thinking about the possibility he was still married to this other woman. No, perhaps this was just some recent girlfriend. That must the answer, she thought to herself. But she had a nagging doubt about the whole business. She decided to confront William the moment he returned from his latest round of business meetings in Laredo.

'But I've filed for divorce. It's no big deal.'

William Nelson was as cool as a cucumber when his pretty young bride confronted him with the evidence. He said that as far as he was concerned, his relationship with Katherine Nelson was over — dead and buried many months previously.

But Omaima was not so sure. Her own naturally inbuilt sense of paranoia was taking over now. She had been scheming all along during her relationship with

William, but now the boot was on the other foot. She had discovered one of his secrets — and it was threatening to put paid to her dreams of an easy life of leisure.

'I don't believe you... you look so happy in the photo.'

'You have to believe me. I wouldn't lie to you.'

But that just wasn't a good enough reply for Omaima. She had been lied to and tricked all through her adult life. Why should she suddenly start trusting someone now? The world was out to get her and she was wreaking her own bizarre form of revenge.

She decided to accept what he was saying, for the moment, while she tried to work out an alternative plan. She knew that if William was still married to Katherine and anything happened to him, then she would get nothing. All those nights of sex she had endured. All those boring evenings listening to him droning on as his whiskey-sodden breath wafted across the table at her. All those awful moments when she pretended to return his lust. It would all turn out to have been a complete waste of time unless he was married to her. Legally.

On the flight back to California they hardly spoke. She was seething with fury. She still feared that he might have another wife. They had long since stopped talking about it, but William Nelson knew full well what his gorgeous young wife was thinking. He appreciated her distress but, as far as he was concerned, she was just a rather insecure young bride.

Over the next two or three weeks, Omaima tried to put the 'other wife' out of her mind as she went about her chores in the Costa Mesa flat. William was often out, working his shady deals, so she took advantage of his absences to stamp her mark on the home they shared.

She had grandiose plans for redecorating the flat, buying better furniture and even laying new beige carpet. But first she set about the task of cleaning it from top to bottom. The trouble was that every few hours she would come across yet more evidence of William's other wife. It was distressing her for all the wrong reasons, and she was starting to wonder if Katherine Nelson had ever visited her husband at that very same apartment, even though William insisted they had been apart for a long period of time.

Every night William came home she would cook him a huge meal but the sparkle had definitely gone out of their relationship. She found it difficult to talk to him and he was well aware that she was still mad at him because of Katherine.

It was about four weeks after their wedding that Omaima realised she could not stand to live a lie any longer. As she cleaned up the apartment yet again and awaited the return of the man she had thought was going to be her saviour just one short month earlier, she felt a surge of fury building through her body like nothing she had ever experienced before. It was even worse than the way she had felt when she attacked Robert Hanson a year earlier in Huntington Beach.

When William Nelson put his key in the front door of their flat as he arrived home that evening, it was like a signal to Omaima. She grabbed the six-inch carving knife off the work surface and walked straight towards the hallway. As her husband walked in, he froze. The blade was pointing right at him.

Omaima did not bother to wait for him to plead for his life. She plunged the knife right into his chest as he stood there in shock at the sight of his deranged wife. The first stab was delivered with all the strength she could muster. For good measure, she twisted the blade round and round to cause maximum damage. It had the desired effect.

William Nelson collapsed on the floor clutching his stomach, where the wound must have been the size of a tennis ball. Then Omaima calmly stood over him for a moment before looking down in disdain at the writhing bigamist who was now at her complete mercy.

She bent over him and looked deep into his eyes. They were cesspools of fear now. Glazed with terror as he saw the bloodied knife in her hand. At one point he tried to clutch her but ended up swiping through thin air because his sight was misty and unclear.

His attempt to stop her just enflamed her determination to finish him off. She lashed that knife through his shoulder blade. Over and over again she struck. After each wound was inflicted he gasped for air as the bubbles of blood started to come up in his throat. Omaima felt no emotion or pain as she rained that knife down on him. Her only thoughts were to avenge his deception and on how she would get rid of the butchered corpse.

Ornaima tried to keep her eyes averted from the task at hand as she sliced through the tender flesh. She knew that if she looked down at her husband's corpse, then she might be sick. And that would mean more to clear up. As it was, she had him laid out on the floor over plastic bin liners so that the blood did not seep through onto the heads of the tenants in the flat below.

Strangely enough, the longer she was there carving away the easier it became. After dislodging each limb, she placed it in one of the four trash bags she was gradually filling up. In many ways, this was the easy part. Carrying the squelching bags down to the car would be a far riskier operation, as she would inevitably encounter other residents of the apartment complex and that might prove a little tricky.

The head was the last piece of her husband's body to be placed gently in one of those extra strong bin bags. She was surprised by the weight of it. She tried hard not to look at it but she could not resist one glance as she held it right out in front of her so as to avoid getting blood on her dress. He looked oddly content as he stared back at her. There might even have been a smile on his stiff, blue lips. She stopped for a moment and blinked her eyes. It almost seemed as if he had winked at her. It was only when she opened and closed her eyes quickly that she realised it was just an illusion.

As she tied the top of that last bin bag tightly and lifted it up to begin the journey out to her husband's shining red Corvette sports car in the underground garage, she did not even notice the nosy neighbour from across the hall eyeing the drip of blood that was coming from one of the split bags. That same resident had heard a man's screams a few hours earlier but thought nothing of it, as there were quite a few strange people living in the block. But when he saw the bin bags and the blood, he knew something was seriously wrong. His fears were further confirmed when Omaima appeared to have blood still on her arms. The police were on the scene within minutes...

Omaima Nelson is currently being held without bail at the Orange County Jail charged with the murder of her husband. A few weeks after her arrest, in December, 1991, she was also charged with imprisoning and attempting to rob Robert Hanson at the apartment they had shared in Huntington Beach, California.

WOMEN IN CHAINS
True stories of women trapped in lives of genuine slavery
Wensley Clarkson

THE MURDER OF RACHEL NICKELL
The truth about the tragic murder on Wimbledon Common
Mike Fielder

CAGED HEAT
What really goes on behinds the bars of women's prisons
Wensley Clarkson

YOU COULD WIN THE AMAZING
SLEUTH'S SILVER DAGGER!

The first twelve titles in Blake's True Crime Library series each contain a question relating to the book. Collect the numbered editions of Blake's True Crime Library, and when you have the answers to all the questions, fill in the form which you will find at the back of the twelfth book and send it to Blake Publishing to be entered into a prize draw.

HERE IS THE EIGTH QUESTION
What model and colour was Harold Smith's truck?
The winner will receive the exclusive sleuth's silver dagger and five runners-up will receive three free copies of Blake's True Crime Library titles.

How To Enter
Fill in the answer form contained in the twelfth book in the series and post it to us. If you have won, we will notify you. Whether you are a winner or not, you will still be eligible for a *FREE* True Crime newsletter!

Competition Rules
1. The 'How to Enter' instructions form part of the rules.
2. These competitions are not open to any members of Blake Publishing or their families, or Blake Publishing's advertising agents, printers or distributors.
3. The prizes will be awarded in order of their value, to the senders of the first winning entries after the closing date.
4. Entries must be on the entry coupon supplied and will not be accepted after the closing date.
5. No claim is necessary, winners will be notified.
6. In cases where a manufacturer discontinues a product which has been specified as a prize, Blake Publishing Ltd will substitute the nearest equivalent model of similar or higher value.
7. The Editor's decision is final, and no correspondence can be entered into.

BEAT THE RUSH!
ORDER YOUR COPIES OF FORTHCOMING TRUE CRIME TITLES DIRECTLY.

Simply fill in the form below, and we will send you your books as they become available.

Name: ....

Address: ....

....

....

Daytime tel.: ....

Card (please tick as appropriate)

Visa ❒ Mastercard ❒

Access ❒ Switch ❒

Card number: ....

Expiry date: ....

For Switch cards only:

Issue date .... Issue number ....

Please send me *(tick as appropriate)*

❒ Deadlier than the Male
Wensley Clarkson

❒ Natural Born Killers
Kate Kray

❒ In the Company of Killers
Norman Parker

❒ The Spanish Connection
John Lightfoot

❒ Doctors who Kill
Wensley Clarkson

❒ Deadly Affair
Nicholas Davies

❒ Vigilante!
Ron Farebrother with Martin Short

❒ Women in Chains
Wensley Clarkson

❒ The Murder of Rachel Nickell
Mike Fielder

❒ Caged Heat
Wensley Clarkson

All titles are £4.99. Postage and packing are free. No money will be deducted from your card until the books become available.